Praise for Jackson Dean C

Over 100 ★★★★★ ratings on the most
Over 10,000 downloads! Top 10 Horror Fict.

"Jackson Dean Chase has found a place on my shelf, the **dark corner, where I hide my twisted little secrets**." —*Tome Tender*

"...He really **has a way with words that leaves me in awe**..." —*Fang Freakin' Tastic Reviews*

"**Jackson Dean Chase is a master** when it comes to twisted endings..." —Kindle reviewer

"...**One of the best horror writers out there.** He grabs you, holds your attention and then **scares you to death**." —*Kindle reviewer*

"If you're looking for some **thrills and chills**... look no further than Jackson Dean Chase." —*Kindle reviewer*

Praise for the *Post-Apocalypse Writer's Phrase Book:*

"...The **perfect sentences** to **enhance your story**." —*Derek Aisles, author of Zombie Command*

"This is a **very handy tool** for writing of any kind. ...there are **a ton of great ideas**... If you're a writer, content creator, blogger, or just looking to expand your knowledge and vocabulary, this is **a really great piece of work**." —*Kindle reviewer*

"**An amazing book!** A handy guide for any apocalyptic author." —*Kindle reviewer*

"...**A great tool for inspiring writers**." —*Kindle reviewer*

"...Enough phrases to convey **gasp-worthy terror**, **horror**, and steer a tale in any direction..." —*Tome Tender*

"There is a **terrific range of topics** in the book for phrases concerning everything from animals to robots to zombies." —*Kindle reviewer*

"...**A useful tool for any writer** to have in their box of tricks. It's also **a fun read** and a way to **kick start your creative juices**." —*Kindle reviewer*

Praise for the *Horror Writers' Phrase Book*:

"A book of **chilling inspiration**... it's worth your investment." —*Lake Lopez, author Thorns in Dark Places*

"The **perfect guide** for writing horror." —*Derek Ailes, author of Zombie Command*

"Mr. Chase's **handy little book of horrors** will help **jump start** [your] **twisted creativity**... like bouncing ideas around with an author buddy." —*Tome Tender*

"**Good stuff!**" —*Kevin Hale, Live Paranormal Talk Radio host*

"When you get stuck as a writer [Jackson's] books are **useful tools** as prompts." —*Kindle reviewer*

"...**This book has helped me tremendously**. I was ready to trash my manuscript and now I'm halfway through editing the first draft!" —*Kindle reviewer*

"**I got the help I needed** [and] came up with with **a dozen new story ideas**." —*Kindle reviewer*

"...This writer is **passionate** [and] isn't pretentious, unlike other how-to books I have read." —*Kindle reviewer (UK)*

"It's sure to **get your imagination pumping**." —*Kindle reviewer*

"**...a lifesaver to any writer.**" —*Kindle reviewer*

ACTION

WRITERS' PHRASE BOOK

Essential Reference for All Authors of
Action, Adventure & Thrillers

JACKSON DEAN
CHASE

www.JacksonDeanChase.com

— For those who want to live a life worth dying for. —

First Printing, October 2015

ISBN-13: 978-1517770358

ISBN-10: 1517770351

Published by Jackson Dean Chase, Inc.

Printed by CreateSpace

ACTION WRITERS' PHRASE BOOK

Copyright © 2015 Jackson Dean Chase, Inc. All rights reserved.

Cover art by SelfPubBookCovers.com/ktarrier

Author photo by C. Graves. Copyright © 2015 Jackson Dean Chase, Inc.

Without limiting the rights under copyright above, no part of this book may be reproduced, stored in or introduced into a retrieval system or transmitted, in any form or by any means (electronic, mechanical, photocopying, recording, or otherwise), without the written consent of both the copyright holder and the above publisher of this book.

PUBLISHER'S NOTES

"Bold Visions of Dark Places" is a trademark of Jackson Dean Chase, Inc.

All the material herein is presented "as is" with no warranty of fitness given for any specific purpose. Neither the author nor his affiliates, heirs, partners, or publishers assume any responsibility for errors, inaccuracies, or omissions.

The scanning, uploading, and distribution of this book via the Internet or via any other means without the written permission of the publisher is illegal and punishable by law. Please purchase only authorized electronic editions, and do not participate in or encourage electronic piracy of copyrighted materials. Your support of the author is appreciated.

Want FREE books? Visit the Author at:
www.JacksonDeanChase.com

Contents

INTRODUCTION 9
Writing Exercises 11

Part 1: Death and Dying

BLADES
Axes, Hatchets, and Cleavers 14
Broken Glass 17
Chainsaws 18
Knives, Machetes, and Swords 19
Razors and Scalpels 22

BLUDGEONS
Brawling and Martial Arts 25
Crushing Weapons and Objects 28
Mechanized Death 30

BURNING
Burned Alive 33
Electrocution (including Stun Guns and Tasers) 35
Explosives 37
Flamethrowers 39

FUTURISTIC WEAPONS
Drones 41
Electrified 42
Energy 43
Monomolecular 44
Projectile 45
Security Systems 46
Sonic 46
Spring-Loaded 46

GUNS

Aiming and Firing	47
Ammunition and Loading	49
Automatic Weapons	50
Body Hits	52
Gunfights	55
Head Shots	56
Misses	58
Muzzle Flashes	59
Pistols	60
Rifles	61
Silencers	62
Shotguns	63
Tranquilizer Guns	64

IMPALEMENT

Bows and Crossbows	65
Spears, Spikes, and Pointy Things	67

LIQUIDS and VAPORS

Acid	69
Drowning	70
Poison and Gassing	71

STRANGULATION

Hanging and Neck Snaps	73
Strangling by Device	74
Strangling by Hands	75

WOUNDS and CORPSES

Blood and Gore	77
Dead Bodies	79
Decapitation and Head Trauma	82
Dismemberment	84
Eye Injuries	85
Gutting	86
Whips and Torture	88

Part 2: Human Suffering

EMOTIONS

Ambition and Greed 92
Fear and Surprise 93
Hate and Revenge 97
Jealousy and Lust 101
Sadness and Despair 103

PROBLEMS

Alcohol 105
Disease and Disfigurement 106
Drugs 108
Nausea, Fainting, and Vomiting 109

Part 3: Man Against Nature

ELEMENTAL FURY

Cold and Ice 112
Earth and Stone 113
Heat and Flame 114
Night and Shadow 116
Water and Wind 117

WILDLIFE

Animals 120
Bats and Birds 121
Reptiles 122
Vermin 123
Water Predators 124

Part 4: Words of Power

HELL'S COLORING BOOK

Colors 126
Colors Writing Exercise 127

VOCABULARY of DEATH

Acid and Drowning 128
Biting and Blood-Drinking 128
Crushing 128
Cutting and Clawing 128
Fire, Electrocution, Explosions, and Guns 128
Killer and Victim Vocalizations 129
Murder and Execution 129
Piercing 129
Strangling and Fainting 129
Violent Release of Bodily Fluids, Guts, and Organs 130
Violent Removal of Body Parts and Skin 130
Vocabulary Writing Exercise 130

RESOURCES

About the Author 131
More Books by the Author 132
Special Thanks 134

PLEASE READ BEFORE BUYING:

All of the *Writers' Phrase Books* feature overlapping content because they are intended as stand-alone volumes. If you already own the *Horror* or *Post-Apocalypse Writers' Phrase Books*, you should be aware that the *Action Writers' Phrase Book* contains little new content. There are a handful of new and/or revised tags and advice sidebars, including tips on writing effective action scenes, customizing gun tags, and naming futuristic weapons.

So why does this book exist? To reach a new market of authors writing action, adventure, and thrillers. This book strips out all the magic, monsters, and doomsday stuff to give action-focused writers just the tools they need. However, if you create genre mash-ups, the *Horror* or *Post-Apocalypse Phrase Books* offer better value.

You may also be interested in buying a copy of my exciting new guide book, *How to Write Realistic Men: The Top 5 Secrets You Need to Know and What to Do with Them!* It contains important insights into male psychology, how to create credible bonding scenes, and the way we act and talk.

Introduction

I'm going to tell you a secret: *A lot of what you write isn't what you say, it's how you say it.* Sure, characters, story structure, and dialogue are important. There are a ton of books written on those subjects for a reason. But you could be an expert in all those things and still fail to tell a compelling story.

Why? Well, to be a truly great writer, you must constantly find new ways to say the same old things. Let's say you're writing a novel about a a ninja assassin. How many different ways can you think of to describe silently killing a man? Or how that feels? What about describing the weather, the wildlife? Remember, these things are going to come up dozens of times and you've got hundreds of pages to fill!

It doesn't matter if you're writing the next James Bond or Jason Bourne. The same problem applies. Sooner or later, you'll find yourself writing the same descriptions over and over. And you'll agonize over each and every one, wondering how to inject new energy into them. But what if you didn't have to? What if you had an entire book of ready-made tags to inspire you at a moment's notice?

Tag—You're It!

Wait! What are tags, you ask? Tags are short descriptive phrases peppered between the dialogue and strung throughout the narrative. Done with skill, the reader never notices them, but their dramatic resonance is deeply felt. Trust me, your readers will notice if they're missing or not up to snuff!

Consider the difference between saying, "He glared at her and she became afraid," or "His gaze burned with such intensity she felt her soul shiver." Which do you prefer? Which is more exciting? Sure, both get the author's point across, but the second is more likely to leave the reader breathless and scrambling to turn the page.

Tags are like bullets. They are the greatest weapons in a writer's arsenal. The more you have, the more firepower you can bring to bear, blasting boring lines to bits and breathing new life into even the most mundane characters and situations.

INSTANTLY WRITE BETTER ACTION

This book provides the tools you need to get the job done, and takes aim at those writing within the Action, Adventure, and Thriller genres.

Regardless of genre, every story requires building the right atmosphere to create an emotional connection to its reader. Without one, why would anyone care if tough guy Snake Samson gets trapped in the secret base of the terrorist commandos? He'd just be human hamburger like so many cardboard characters in bad novels and B-movies. But if you can get inside Snake's head and really *feel* what it's like to be him, you can make the reader love him, fear for him, and pray he survives the fight.

In the best fiction, whether you make Snake a "throwaway" victim in the prologue or the hero himself, he becomes a stand-in for readers to project themselves into and identify with. Readers *want* to feel his fear, his isolation, the sense of impending doom hanging over him as all hope seems lost. That is what turns what might have been a cheap action scene into a moment of grueling suspense.

So how do we make our example character more meaningful? We assign Snake's thoughts, words, and actions greater power with every tap of our keyboard. In short, we punch him up with tags. And we do the same for the terrorists. And everyone else who matters.

Use your intuition. Not every line needs to be punched-up. After all, sometimes it's perfectly fine (and perhaps even *more* dramatic in a minimalist sense) to say, "He shot him," instead of "The bullet blazed through bone, spattering brains in a crimson mist."

Nor is it wise for every act, thought or description to be over-the-top or made to stick out unnecessarily. But when you want to really emphasize something, to build atmosphere and heighten emotion, nothing beats a well-written tag. Use them right, use them well, and your stories will never be the same.

HOW DO I USE THIS BOOK?

At the very least, just flipping through these pages should jumpstart your creative juices, especially if you've come down with a bad case of writer's block. You can use the tags as writing prompts to help you generate new scenes or even entire stories, but the most common method is to use them as quick "fill in the blanks" whenever you need a line. You have my permission to copy them "as is," or customize them however you like.

Some tags are more specific than others, so you may find it helpful to swap out whatever doesn't work for you with whatever you need. For example, changing the gender of the character or type of weapon and/or action is easily done, as is replacing the generic pronouns given with your character's names or some other vivid description instead (e.g., changing "the man" to "the cruel killer").

You can achieve a variety of exciting effects by mixing and matching tags (or parts of tags) from the same or different categories to create new ones. Say you need to describe Snake seeing a tiger for the first time and your mind draws a blank. Simply flip to the "Man Against Nature" section, then to "Animals." Scan the listed tags until you find one you like, then use it "as is," combine it with others to come up with completely new ones.

For example, you could combine "The tiger was a flashing nightmare of black and orange," and "The lion unsheathed its killing claws," to become "The tiger was a nightmare of killing claws."

So you not only have all the individual tags as written, but you also have an incredible number of combinations—a number limited only by your imagination. There's no wrong way to use this book except not to use it all. *It's yours.* Feel free to tinker with it. Mark it up, write in the margins, but whatever you do, have fun!

— **Jackson Dean Chase**

www.JacksonDeanChase.com

— How To Exterminate Weak Writing —

Here are three easy exercises designed to seek and destroy slothful descriptions. Pick a category or subcategory of tags that you know will be important to your story, especially a subject you feel you're weak on (such as "Wildlife" if you're writing a jungle adventure).

Exercise #1: Read all the listed tags from your category or subcategory, making note of the top ten tags you like and the bottom ten you don't. Now challenge yourself to revise, combine, or otherwise alter all ten of your favorite tags, then do the same to improve your least favorite ones.

Exercise #2: Combine parts of tags from one category with those from another, mixing-and-matching as best you can to create new effects. For example, a specific headshot from "Guns" could be combined with a kill from "Decapitation and Head Trauma." You could take this one step further, using an entirely different weapon (such as an axe), or maybe even making the head explode or be torn off by a mutant or psychic attack.

Exercise #3: Challenge yourself to come up with at least ten totally original tags on your favorite subject. Dig deep, and feel the gates of inspiration open!

Books by Jackson Dean Chase

Fiction

Beyond the Dome series:
- #0 Hard Times in Dronetown
- #1 Drone
- #2 Warrior (coming soon)

Young Adult Horror series:
- #1 Come to the Cemetery
- #2 The Werewolf Wants Me
- #3 The Haunting of Hex House
- #4 Gore Girls: Twisted Tales & Poems
- #5 Lost Girls: Twisted Tales & Poems
- #6 Horror Girls: Twisted Tales & Poems
- #7 Killer Young Adult Fiction (complete series + extras)

Non-Fiction

How to Write Realistic series:
- #1 How to Write Realistic Men
- #2 How to Write Realistic Women (coming soon)

Writers's Phrase Book series:
- #1 Horror Writers' Phrase Book
- #2 Post-Apocalypse Writers' Phrase Book
- #3 Action Writers' Phrase Book
- #4 Fantasy Writers' Phrase Book (coming soon)

— Part 1 —
Death and Dying

— BLADES —

Axes, Hatchets, and Cleavers

The axe cleaved, death riding in its wake

The axe made a red ruin of his chest

The axe chopped down with savage fury

The deadly axe crunched home

The big blade buried itself in his skull

The axe's silver head sang, severing life from limb

A man's weapon, the weight of the axe felt good in his hand

His head burst like a ripe melon beneath the killer's axe

Axe clutched firmly in hand, he set off into the night

The fire axe hung loosely in his hand, a grim reminder of death

Her hands hefted the heavy axe with a sureness her mind did not share

The heavy axe chopped their struggling limbs like kindling

The axe became stuck in the wound and would not pull free

The hungry axe feasted on brain and bone

With one swing of the axe, their nightmare began

The heavy chop brutalized his foe, driving him back

The axe laid his ribcage open, exposing meat and bone

He shook the dripping gristle from the head of his axe

The vicious swing chunked into his chest, bursting organs

A weapon of war, the battleaxe was born to cleave flesh from bone

The only closure for him came at the end of an axe

With one mighty blow, he brought the axe home

The deadly axe screamed down, sending up a shower of blood

He shook the axe to dislodge sticky clumps of brain and bone

The axe chopped his neck as easily as cordwood

The axe's razored edge cried out for blood

The honed edge tore through her clothes to find the flesh beneath

The axe split her pregnant belly open in a shower of gore

The axe chopped relentlessly at the bound victim

With a sickening crunch, he wrenched the axe free from the wound

The two men fought over the axe, each grabbing hold of the handle

The axe fell from nerveless fingers as the killer collapsed

He growled and raised his axe to the bruised and purpling sky

The heavy axe embedded itself in the wall

The axe crashed into the door, splintering wood

He bashed in her skull with the broken axe handle and called it a day

He hurled the axe, desperate to strike

The honed hatchet flew from his fist

The hurled hatchet bit through bone, crushing ribs

A hatchet in each hand, he looked ready for war

He pulled a razor-sharp hand axe from his belt clip

The spinning tomahawk came straight for him

Cold steel tumbling end over end, the hand axe came

A calling card of death, the throwing axe delivered itself into his chest

Meat cleaver raised high, the killer charged

The cleaver chopped through his chest

The cleaver broke through bone

The dripping cleaver danced from limb to limb, singing its mad chorus

The butcher's blade bit into the meat of his neck

The cleaver began its grisly work, butchering them like human hogs

The cleaver chopped the screaming children to pieces

The flashing cleaver thudded into him

The cold steel cleaver crashed into her face and hung there

No butcher ever wielded a blade like that

The hungry cleaver chomped on his neck

The dripping cleaver spattered the slaughterhouse floor

He shook the savage cleaver and a red rain fell from it

He swung the meat cleaver in a vicious chopping motion

The bloody cleaver slashed and chopped

Where the butcher's blade fell, only spurting stumps remained

The cleaver-crushed skull spilled brains like a grisly *piñata*

The butcher's arm grew tired and the bloody cleaver dropped to his side

The murderous cleaver clattered to the kitchen floor

The madman's cleaver hacked him to pieces

— USE TAGS WITH ANY TIME PERIOD —

Remember, while many of the weapon tags are obviously of medieval or modern origin, as long as an equivalent weapon exists in your setting, you can change the tags to fit whatever time period you need. For example, if your story takes place in the far future, you can change swords to "plasma sabers," chainsaws to "robo-rippers," and guns to "laser pistols" or "blaster rifles." For historical or fantasy, change grenades to "Greek fire," guns to "wands," even vehicles can become "chariots," "wagons," "carriages," or some form of steampunk or magic equivalent.

Broken Glass

The broken bottle was better than no weapon at all

The broken bottle raked out

The broken bottle caught her throat

The emerald bottle slashed deep

The broken bottle turned his face into a crimson mask

She used the broken bottle to ward the men off

He smashed the bottle, making it into a makeshift blade

He drew back the bottle and the wound became a pulsing fountain

Broken glass gashed and gouged

Jagged glass punched fragile flesh

The glass cut through air, then flesh

The glass drew a savage red line across her pale throat

Broken glass became hungry teeth in the hands of the mob

He punched the mirror and pulled back a dripping red fist

She smashed the mirror and snatched up a shard to defend herself

She wrapped cloth around the shard's end to protect her hand

The shard of broken mirror sank into his unprotected neck

Broken glass bit into her bare feet

Broken glass crunched underfoot, drawing blood

He crashed through the window, cutting himself badly

The window shrapneled into a thousand deadly shards

Glittering shards rained from the broken skylight

The stained glass exploded in a rainbow of death

Jackson Dean Chase

Chainsaws

The chainsaw shaved off his head

He dragged the chainsaw across her neck and laughed

Gushing red, the chainsawed corpse toppled to the barn floor

The chainsaw carved him like a Thanksgiving roast

In a cloud of smoke, the chainsaw whirled and danced

He swung the smoking machine into her path and revved it

The screaming blade sliced him in hall

The buzzing blade savaged her soft, white throat

He swung the chainsaw down, butchering the dog as it came for him

The saw showered him with red as he savaged her again and again

Where the blade buzzed, death followed

The machine took his arm off and sent it flying

The saw cut the air with a hungry whine

The growling blade gashed open his guts

The saw left a mutilated mess on the barn floor

The saw left a leaking pile of guts and gore where life had been

The revving blade spat death

Metal teeth took her arm off at the elbow

The saw's hungry teeth caught in his flesh and chewed noisily

The saw's teeth stripped flesh from bone

The saw tore his head off in a cloud of smoke and gore

The saw left a jagged stump spurting red

Whatever the saw touched, it took

Caught in its merciless teeth, all she could do was die

The hungry teeth ground into flesh

The hellish blade's hunger demanded human meat

In his hateful hands, the saw screamed revenge

The chainsaw chopped down, chewing meat

The spinning blade was savage in its butchery

The brutal blade buzzed and smoked

The stench of gas and spilled guts accompanied the buzzing of the saw

The saw spoke in a buzzing tone that promised death

Knives, Machetes, and Swords

He saw the splash of blood even before he knew he'd been stabbed

He saw the splash of blood even before he knew he'd been stabbed

The knife squished home

The knives worked—slicing, stabbing, cutting until no life was left

The knife was a crimson stinger and hate was its venom

The knife stabbed down and left him convulsing on the floor

The blade stuck out of him and he staggered back

The knife cut his vocal chords before he could scream

The knife let the air out of his lung and he wheezed back, frothing gore

The blade poked in, pressing hard and pricking a lung

The finely-honed blade ripped through the guard's larynx

n his flesh, the bayonet found what bullets could not

In his flesh, the bayonet found what bullets could not

Cold combat steel plunged into his side

He took six-inches of steel in his gut

He cleaned the dripping survival knife on his victim's clothes

The hunting knife skewered his hand to the table

The hunting knife whispered from its sheath

The short-bladed knife sprang from its leather sheath

He slid the folded knife into his boot

The cruel butcher knife glittered in her slim hand

The electric carving knife buzzed off chunks of still-living morsels

He took an electric carving knife to her screaming face

The butterfly knife clacked open in his hand

The butterfly knife sprang steely wings, revealing the concealed blade

One flick of his thumb extended the switchblade a wicked five-inches

He thumbed the switchblade's trigger

The slim knife glittered in her hand, hinting death

She made a quick gesture with the switchblade at the guy's crotch

The ritual dagger's curved blade sprang like a serpent

The dagger of death plunged down in sacrifice

The wavy-bladed dagger feasted on the sacrifice of virgin flesh

The dagger slid between bloodied ribs, seeking vital organs

The dagger drank his life's blood

The dagger in her hand promised death

A deadly dagger clawed the air

The throwing knife flicked from her hand and found its mark

The throwing knife flew from practiced fingers

The knife came out of nowhere, thunking into the wall beside him

The murderous machete chopped human meat

The machete hacked the handsome face into gory garbage

The machete slashed though the arm as easily as hacking brush

The savage machete took off her head at the neck

A crimson fountain rained from where the machete had been

Death spurted from the wound as the machete completed its deadly arc

And in the swing of that sword, his nightmare ended

Her sword kissed his throat

The sword swung in a vicious arc, cleaving all who came before it

The savage blow sent him reeling—half one way, half the other

The sword sliced down, ending his screams

His blade tore the enemy open in a fountain of flashing red

The clash of cold steel called him to battle

His blade thirsted for enemy blood

Their swords clashed in a mighty clang that shook the castle walls

In his expert hands, the sword sang sweet songs of death

The sword sang its silvery death song

The sword's song was death and he, its conductor

The sword flew from its scabbard

The blade tore free from its scabbard

The blade felt good in his hand, as did the deaths that followed

Her slim blade flashed in a practiced arc

His blade was long, his memory longer still

His blade drank deep of the gushing red fountain

He shook the gore from his blade

The bloody blade made short work of him

The first cut was an appetizer to the feast of death that followed

Cold steel caressed the wound

Cold steel bit into him, bringing with it the comfort of death

The sword swung in savage fury

His sword cut a crimson swath through the attackers

Her swinging blade chopped into the fallen man's groin, castrating him

The sword-savaged flesh fell away from the blow in two dripping pieces

His sword formed a whirling wall of death before him

The swing sliced his torso open and he stumbled back in a splash of red

The long blade came around in a powerful arc

Steel met steel as the swordsmen fought

He jabbed the thin blade of the fencing foil forward

He parried the blow with his own sword and counterattacked

— WHAT TYPE OF SWORD IS IT? —

While technically all swords are "swords," different types of swords exist and they are used differently in battle.

For example, both the German *zweihander* and Scottish claymore are massive two-handed swords built for chopping foes down. They are deadly, but heavy and slow.

Compare that to the nimble Japanese *katana* (better known as the samurai sword). It is useful for both slashing and piercing, and can be wielded either one- or two-handed.

The French *rapier* is a thin, one-handed fencing blade used for duels. The user makes quick, thrusting attacks to pierce his enemy.

Knowing a weapon's type and the kind of motions its wielder must make to successfully attack or defend will help you write credible combat scenes.

Razors and Scalpels

The razor had done its work

The razor ripped across her neck

She clutched the straight razor and prayed he would come

The straight razor unfolded in his hand, a glittering promise of pain

Cold steel razored the air

Blood burst from the razor wounds in flowing red agony

The razor whispered across her throat

The ghastly razor sliced through the pale ivory of her skin

Wherever the razor's steel touched, blood bloomed in crimson flowers

The playful razor nicked him, a foretaste of death

Her jealous razor was greedy for his blood

He ran his razor over her carotid artery

The razor kissed her neck

Red horror splashed down her dress as the razor ripped free

The razor ravaged his throat

The razor ripped and ravaged

Razor ripped flesh spat streams of savage red matter

A flash of silver and her throat spilled open, hot and sticky

The hellish razor drank deep from the pulsing juices of life

The maniac tossed the scalpel between his hands, taunting us to take it

The razor whispered the poetry of death to her throbbing veins

She ran the razor blade over her wrists and leaned back in the tub

The straight razor severed the jugular in a violent spray of gushing red

The bathwater turned ruby-red from the razor's work

A red rain washed from the razor's wound

Black blood pulsed in inky spurts from the bone-deep cut

She pressed the blade home to end her pain

She had cut herself many times, but never like this

Glittering death flashed from the surgeon's blade

A scalpel in his hand, the mad doctor prescribed death

The scalpel slid easily into her soft flesh

His scalpel made a living autopsy of the girl's struggling body

He snatched up a scalpel from the surgical table

The scalpel cut him to the bone

Scalpel in hand, the psychotic nurse lunged

The surgeon's tool sliced deep

The scalpel knifed toward her throat

A ruby line blushed where the scalpel had touched

The scalpel slivered her open from stem to stern

The scalpel swiveled in his hand, twisting the wound wide

All business, the coroner cut into the corpse

The scalpel drew a vivid red line from pubic bone to clavicle

The scalpel met his neck in a scarlet symphony

The surgeon's blade slashed, parting her throat in a sticky red sea

BLUDGEONS

Brawling and Martial Arts

He hit hard and strong

He hit fast and fierce

He backhanded her across the face

He rained down a flurry of blows

A hairy fist cracked against his jaw

The punch left him reeling, spitting teeth

He landed a lucky blow

Her red nails raked his cheek, clawing for the eyes

He knocked the guy out with a good right to the jaw

A sucker-punch took him upside the head, sending him sprawling

One kick and he doubled over in pain as she laughed

She kneed him and he went down grunting

He reeled under the lightning blows

One more punch would finish him

The man's hairy fist knocked the wind out of her

The devastating blow sent her sprawling to the ground

His fists left her face a disfigured mask

She landed a lucky blow and dazed her attacker

His hairy knuckles slid across the man's jaw with a meaty *thwack!*

A massive fist impacted against his temple, sending him sprawling

The giant's sure grip crushed him in a deadly bear-hug

He felt his ribs grate under that lethal grip

He sank his thumb into a flaring nostril, ripped and pulled

The bodyguard clotheslined him, one arm catching across his chest

He smashed her across the face in a frenzy

The girl's knee took him by surprise

She kicked, bit and scratched viciously

Manicured talons dug into the tender flesh of his groin and twisted

The big man tumbled down, unconscious

He cracked her across the face for good measure

She slapped him hard, determined in her defiance

He whipped his elbow around and drove the point into his jaw

The knob of bone crashed into his mouth

His foot stomped holy hell out of her hide

Her lanky leg kicked out, driving into his midsection

He hooked his leg around the man and slammed him to the floor

Hands clawed at her hair and came away with a bloody clump of scalp

He kicked him hard in the jaw, dazing him

He knotted up his fists and launched a pair of brutal strokes

He snapped his right knee up at the attacker

He brought down his boot on the creep's throat with merciless force

His boot stomped down, crushing windpipe and smashing vertebrae

Vomit spewed from her red lips as his boot drove into her guts

Her stiletto heel dug into his neck, then disappeared in a splash of red

He wore a heavy ring that opened up a ragged gash beneath her eye

The open-handed blow stunned her into silence—but not submission

Hate-hardened fists beat a bruising tattoo across his midsection

The nose pulped, the fingers smashed, and still the beating continued

The professional beating sent him into a screaming purple agony

Ugly purple bruises were forming all over his body from the beating

His judo-hardened hands knifed out in lethal chops

The roundhouse kick crashed into his chest

A quick chop to the neck was all it took

All her training paid off in one blow

Her foot met his face in a crunch of bone that knocked his teeth in

He formed his right hand into a lethal plane

The inside edge of the stiffened hand caught him just below the jaw line

His stiffened hand swung in a slashing motion

His skilled hands chopped the air like blades of death

He lashed out with two quick left kicks

Ruthless fists and kicks from years of training connected with him now

He pounded the hell out of the guy, stomping ribs and smashing teeth

One hand beckoned, daring his enemy to come to him

The grinning black-belt moved in for the kill

He circled his opponent like a shark smelling blood

Karate-fueled kicks and chops collided with his gut and ribs

Hairy knuckles crashed home, knocking her senseless

He staggered back from the blow, holding his head and seeing stars

Punch after punch, the big man fought on

When the knockout finally came, the punch sent him into merciful black

Crushing Weapons and Objects

The hammer caved in his skull

The killer pulled the hammer's claw back, cracking him like an eggshell

The sledgehammer swung, crushing everything in its path

The sledgehammer pounded his skull into grisly paste

The flail's spiked ball and chain crashed into his skull

The heavy head of the knight's mace caved in the warrior's skull

The baseball bat hit a bloody home run across his face

The bat hit a grand slam upside his head

The brass knuckles beat him bloody

The 2x4 cracked against his jaw, shattering it

The nightstick left a bloody knot on his head

The cop's billy club left him a mass of bruises and broken bones

Shattered bone sent shockwaves of pain screaming down every nerve

He clobbered him with the bat and ran for his life

He pummeled him with the sticky red bat until the wood cracked

Bloody clumps of hair and scalp were stuck to the improvised club

He swung the table leg as a bludgeon to warn us back

The blackjack's blow emptied her mind into dreamless black

The homemade sap left him sprawled senseless on the living room floor

He reeled back from the weapon's bludgeoning blow

The crowbar crunched down with blinding force

The crowbar dented his skull

The crowbar took him in the forehead, ripping open a ragged furrow

The smashing wound left him blinded him with his own blood

The heavy flashlight brained him

He beat her with the heavy rock her til he could no longer lift his arm

He pried the boulder loose and sent it hurtling down to crush them

The landslide rained down, crushing man and beast alike

The stone's weight smashed down, crushing the life out of him

He hurled a fist-sized rock at the man's head

The rock rammed into the man's skull with a meaty *splat*

The rock crashed off the man's temple, sending him sprawling

With one hateful toss, the dusty brick pulped nose and smashed teeth

The brick bounced off the man's jaw

He brought the rock down, pulping flesh, breaking bone

The rock came away, leaving a bloody crater where her mouth had been

The maddened hooves of the cattle stampeded over him

He was trampled into dirt and dust by a hundred hooves

A heavy hoof sent snapping, jolting pain up his body

The world rushed up to meet him as he fell

The pavement took him in a red asphalt embrace

The body burst on impact, splattering the pavement hot red

The asphalt beckoned with the gravity of death

Like a hungry black snake, the street rose up to meet the falling man

The body crashed into the roof of the parked car with a sticky *thud*

With a heavy heart, she joined the crashing waves and rocks far below

He stepped out onto the ledge and stared at the street below

As he stepped off the ledge, he felt a kind of freedom

Jackson Dean Chase

Mechanized Death

The hellish machine ground him to hamburger

The gears ground him down, then out

What the machine spit out resembled nothing human

The vise trapped her head and deformed it like a sideshow freak

In the blink of an eye, the machine had him

The gears gobbled him and he was gone

The man crumpled across the hood of the car

He stepped in front of the speeding train and was gone

Tied to the train tracks, she struggled to free herself

The subway train smashed her to pieces

What the train trampled, no doctor could put back together again

The steamroller paved him into a human pancake

The bus ground the child under its wheels for an entire city block

The body became a mangled wreck under those eighteen wheels

His eyes went wide as the machine bore down on him

The truck jackknifed and careened toward the gas station

The truck took him for a ride under its wheels

The semi pulped him to paste at sixty miles an hour

The big eighteen-wheeler smashed into him

He became pulped paste under those eighteen wheels

A horror of pulped brains and ground meat slid off the wheel

The flattened face wept eyes and teeth from the heavy wheel

Blood and bones became grisly Jell-O as the big rig paved over him

Action Writers' Phrase Book

Pulped brains dripped off the big rig's wheels

The car made the child a crimson smear that cried no more

An oil slick of blood greased the highway

Black rubber left a bloody trail behind the fleeing vehicle

The old woman rode over the windshield, frail as match sticks

The blind old fool was going to run us down

He didn't even honk, just hit him, and kept on going

The car hit fast, but death came slow

The icy road ripped the car's control out from under him

A madman sat behind the wheel, his brain humming death

She flew through the shattered windshield into the night

Oblivious, he backed into the plane's propeller and became pink mist

The tire collapsed in a hissing rumble

The Jeep faltered badly, then went over the cliff

He fought the skid, losing control as the car drifted wide

The Devil himself could not have driven that car any better

He pushed the witness off the curb and into an early grave

Nothing screamed "accident" more than a failed brake line

The child became a bloody smear across my windshield

The whole point of "hit and run" was to get away with it

He tapped the brakes, only to find they'd been cut

The car sailed over the cliff onto the uncaring rocks below

The car cruised off the pier into death's silent waters

The driver panicked and swerved into a tree

He slammed his brakes on black ice and sent the car into a tailspin

He pumped the accelerator and headed for the cliff

I hit the gas, then him

The bumper took him low and hard, rolling him over the hood

The old lady flew over the windshield, an airborne sack of broken bones

I tried to brake, but too late

The cars crashed in a grinding shriek, then burst into flame

The wheels of death paved over his life

The hot rubber of death left tire tracks on his soul

The car crushed him, smashed him out of existence

The impact threw her into a ditch to lie bleeding like roadkill

The black van ran them down while the driver laughed

They threw the girl in the van and backed over her crippled brother

The van hit him at sixty miles an hour

The van plowed through the people in the street

The punks threw him out of the van at top speed

The van slammed through the shop window and into the customers

---

— WHAT TYPE OF VEHICLE IS IT? —

Spice up your vehicle descriptions with the make and model, as well as their color and any other identifying details, such as: racing stripes, flames, a missing license plate, cracked windshield, etc. Establish these facts when the vehicle is first introduced. Knowing these details not only gives the vehicle more personality, but says something about the driver. Is he rich or poor? Reckless or careful?

However, don't get too enamored of your dream car. If you always refer to the hero's car by its full name, such as "Snake got behind the wheel of his red Ferrari 458 Italia," you may get a rosy glow imagining it, but your readers will quickly become annoyed. You want to vary what you call the vehicle, but not too much or too often. Often, simply calling a car a "car" is the right choice.

BURNING

Burned Alive

The gas-soaked man went up in flames

Smoke and ashes, soot and cinders—that is what the victims became

Flame-blackened, the smoking killer lumbered forward

Her body was ash that crumbled at my touch

They were burned beyond recognition, yet somehow lived on

The flames consumed him utterly and not a moment too soon

All the fires of hell wouldn't be enough to claim his evil soul

The fire melted what little humanity remained in his twisted face

Red, yellow, orange: these were the colors of my hate

I shoved him into the oven

A madman with a melted face danced in the firelight of his own demise

The bonfire roared up under her as she screamed

Crackling doom devoured her, body and soul

Caught in the inferno, the people danced and howled and died

Charred by flame, all she could do was laugh madly as she died

Wherever the flame had touched, the flesh hung off him in strips

Her body was one big blister, angry from the heat

The coals shot red-hot knives of crimson fire into his feet

Like moths, the fire extinguished them with its hellish light

A living torch, the man ran to the cliff and fell to the rocks below

A flaming scarecrow staggered from the wreckage

A human comet streaked from the blaze

The flames swallowed hero and villain alike

The hungry flames devoured him

What the flames didn't devour, the shrapnel ate

Cremated corpses scorched the earth from that hellish blast

Bodies became flame-blackened mummies within seconds

The fireball consumed a dozen men, cleaving limbs, shredding flesh

Napalm clung to him, streaming liquid fire

The napalm blistered the villagers to the bone

All around, the sticky napalm burned and roared

Glowing scarlet-yellow, the flames climbed toward our hiding place

Burning doom and blasting ruin, the flames crept closer

All around us, the ghastly inferno raged

Flames licked at her feet like all the hungry devils of hell

A hellfire of living death raged over his body, charring him black

Orange flames ate the screaming face until it screamed no more

Her flesh blistered at the flame's searing touch

The flesh seared off him in seconds

All that was left of the man was charred, smoking meat

She became a human candle of sizzling fat and cooked flesh

Red-hot hell consumed the apartments and all who dwelled within

Flames wrapped the enemy like presents at the devil's birthday party

Wreathed in flames, the killer dived off the pier and disappeared

The corpse's fat bubbled like molten pus

They were human barbecue served up to Satan's oven

Electrocution (Stun Guns, Tasers, etc.)

The switch flipped and a million shuddering volts slammed into him

The stench of ozone sizzled the air

The shock of the cattle prod burned her with more than shame

The deadly current made him a shaking, seizing puppet of death

His eyes popped and mouth foamed as the current juiced through him

A million volts made his eyes melt and head smoke

The electrodes sizzled, her flesh cooked, and the screams began

Every nerve screamed, every muscle contracted as the energy took over

The lightning transfixed him, a burning bolt of blue-white death

The current paralyzed him

No sound escaped the prison of the electrocuted man's mouth

Blazing sparks spit death from the writhing power line

The ruthless current played him like a puppet master

Shuddering, shivering death shot from the power line

The deadly *zzzt!* of electrical current sluiced through his system

Sparks danced over the twitching body

The spitting power cable sent his body into smoking convulsions

Burning bolts of blistering death covered him

He was covered in dazzling, dancing lights that burned and destroyed

The deadly current zapped through him

A million deadly volts shot through him

Electric agony played over every inch of her flesh

Electric fire lit him up like a Christmas tree of death

The lightning bolt shattered into him

Crisping, crackling pain powered through her body

She hit the electric fence and convulsed

The man gripped the electric fence and couldn't let go

The smoking body hung from the electric fence and twitched no more

The cattle prod shocked and seared her flesh

A jolt from the cattle prod convinced him to move

The stun gun crackled and clicked

I pressed the stun gun into his side and thumbed the trigger

The stun gun shocked him senseless

The Taser fired two dart-like electrodes into the man

The civilian Taser's range was limited to fifteen feet

The maximum range of the military Taser was thirty-five feet

The Taser's barbs sent current slamming into his body

The taser's barbs bounced off the maniac's thick, puffy winter coat

Military Tasers could penetrate thick clothes earlier models could not

This newer models had a built-in camera to record taser incidents

The Tasered man jerked and twitched, then fell over

The enraged man ignored the Taser's pain and charged the officer

Tasered, all she could do was grunt and clench her fists

Every muscle contracted against her will

Every muscle screamed

Every muscle clenched impossibly tight

Muscles screaming in spasm, the Tasered man ceased his attack

The shock sent the suspect into spasms

Every muscle in her body was under his electronic control

Unfired or empty Tasers could still cause pain with "Drive Stun" mode

"Drive Stun" mode caused pain without incapacitation

Explosives

His fist squeezed the plastic explosive into a deadly ball

He fed them a steady diet of grenades til Death's appetite was satisfied

He pulled the pin, counted five, and threw

He lobbed the grenade down the hallway

The grenade sailed into the crowd

He lobbed the frag grenade with a practiced hand

He fed the room a pair of Hell's pineapples

A miniature volcano erupted as the grenade fragged him to pieces

A looping, overhand gesture sent the grenade sailing into the crowd

Pulling the pin with his teeth, he hurled the grenade

M34 grenades sent white phosphorus whooshing down the aisle

White phosphorus explosions sprayed fire, torching flesh to the bone

With a *whumph*, the missile streaked from the grenade launcher

He pumped a fresh round into the rifle's grenade launcher

He squeezed the trigger of his firing stick, sending missiles screaming

The chopper shot twin messengers of death at the target

With a deadly *whoosh*, the helicopter launched its missiles

The chopper fired its payload in a blazing barrage

The missiles vaporized everything that lived

Missiles engulfed the building in the screaming fires of hell

There was a deadly *crump* of exploding flame as the missile hit

Warheads belched from bazookas, erupting in giant fireballs

Streaking doom raced from the bazooka

A bazooka blast shook the earth overhead, raining fire and rocks

The bazooka blew the opposition away like leaves on the wind

He lit the dynamite and waited for the fuse to burn down

The dynamite stick came sailing over the old stone wall

The dynamite was old, sweaty, unstable

The fuse sparked in his hand

The dynamite stick was devil-red, holding the promise of hellfire

The bomb blew a hole in him the size of my fist

The bomb blast sent body parts flying

He thumbed the detonator, and the building became a smoky inferno

With a fateful click, the landmine activated

The deadly nitro jostled in the glass with every bump and blunder

The room erupted in an explosion

The doors blew open with a smoky thunderclap

The front steps erupted into flying chunks of stone and tumbling bodies

The burning door burst open on its hinges

Hellfire roared in that awful furnace, bringing damnation and death

He thumbed the triggering device and the world exploded

The massive blast shook the building

The explosion rained crimson hellfire

The blast singed his face

The shock wave blew over him

The frag bomb blew, lifting the truck off its wheels

A series of explosions lifted the burning trucks off their wheels

Hunks of metal ripped away in a fiery mess

The car's gas tank ignited in a hot mushroom cloud

The raging wall of fire rose higher, fueled by ruptured fuel tanks

The flaming hulk of the Ford sped toward him, trailing greasy smoke

Driver and vehicle became one in an angry cloud of red-orange fire

Razored shrapnel cut through the smoke-filled air

The fuel tank ignited like liquid thunder

When the fuel tank blew, it was like a Sunday-school picture of hell

The fireball built toward the sky

An exploding *whump* of fire flushed his face

The propane tank burst, bathing them in orange death

Flamethrowers

Burned and blasted bodies baked under the flamethrower's heat

A tongue of orange fire shot from the flamethrower's barrel

The flamethrower spat and streamed liquid fire into the bunker

The flamethrower's barrel spilled liquid death

The flamethrower hosed them down with orange fire

It licked its tongue of fire across the room

Twin lines of fire belched from the flamethrowers into the crowd

The ignited weapon hissed into life with a savage blue flame

The flamethrower was hungry to kill, burn, destroy

The Nazi *flamenwerfer* swept the trench clean of living flesh

Liquid fire roared from the flamethrower's orange eye

The flamethrower spat blistering doom

A flamethrower caught him, crisping him into an early grave

The flame gun turned the man into a human torch

The flame gun whooshed orange death at the attackers

A shower of flame shot from the burn gun

A whoosh of deadly fire streaked from the gun

An incinerating rain of liquid fire squirted from it

It had an eye like an oven and an appetite from hell

The weapon's tip glowed blue, then spat death

A blazing shower rained from the weapon's nozzle

Wherever the soldier pointed, the flames followed

The flamethrower blazed, blanketing them in its fury

The weapon belched flame

Flame licked from the weapon's nozzle like a hungry dragon

The fuel tank ran out before the carnage was done

The bullet hit the flamethrower's fuel tank, causing it to explode

---

— FLAMETHROWERS IN A QUARANTINE ZONE —

The military will be quick to employ flamethrowers to burn plague-infected bodies. The corpses may be placed in a nearby pile or driven to a pit for disposal. If your hero's friends or family are among the dead, it can make for a tense scene as he races against time to steal back his loved ones' bodies and give them a "proper burial" despite the risks. Whether or not he's successful is up to you. *The Last Man on Earth* (1964) has such a scene.

— Futuristic Weapons —

Drones

The drone crashed through the window and exploded

The drone's rotors chopped through his hands and into his face

Above, I heard the deadly whine of rotors—the drones were coming

The drone hovered overhead, reporting back to its master

He piloted the drone up to her window and watched her undress

The drone was mounted with tranq projectors to subdue its prey

The drone self-destructed, taking half the room with it

Drones flew overhead, watching our every move

I looked out the window and saw a drone staring back at me

The drone dropped its payload of poison gas

The drone flew low, targeting our vehicle

A drone hovered nearby, cameras swiveling in all directions

The drone took damage and wouldn't respond to his commands

The drone lifted from the ground in a whisper of rotors

There was no privacy from the drones, nor any hope of escape

The drone sailed overhead, seeking targets

The drone could not fit through the narrow opening

Pursued by drones, our only escape was the sewer

The drones reported any infractions back to Security

The drone fired its guns in a sustained burst

The damaged drone crashed to the earth

Electrified (also see Electrocution)

The new stun technology was favored by law enforcement—and slavers

The slaver's stun gloves caught her in their electrified grip

He reached out with his stun gauntlets to subdue the prisoner

One touch from the shock gloves sent him reeling to the bunker floor

The robo-spear's tip crackled with energy

The stun-staff knocked him down—and out

The cop's stun baton rendered the criminal senseless

He brought the stun-baton down, knocking the thief out

Stunners or "S-guns" shot electric beams to incapacitate targets

The stunner hit him with enough volts to send him to the floor

The stunner overloaded his central nervous system

The stunner's e-beam crackled into her

The slaver's e-beam sizzled into her soft flesh

Overcome by e-beams, he crumpled to the dirt

Energy (also see Guns)

The laser's focusing crystal was damaged and would no longer fire

Orange bolts cut the air *(substitute laser color of your choice)*

Orange death blazed all around *(substitute laser color of your choice)*

I slapped in a fresh battery pack to reload

Energy bolts cut through the darkness

The beam bounced off the robot's armor

The laser blackened and scorched the tank's armor

Action Writers' Phrase Book

Lasers lit up the night

The steady whine of his laser cut through the noise of the crowd

The laser cannon could fire multiple bolts per second

Laser cannons blasted and burned the invaders

The megablaster was like a laser machine-gun

The megablaster ripped through the enemy ranks

The pulse-ripper was a laser shotgun, deadly at close-range

The pulse-gun sprayed energy

The pulse-gun burned thirty holes in him before he could move

The maser fired electrical beams produced from amplified microwaves

With a crackling hum, the photon maser focused and fired

The weird gun fired green bolts of superheated plasma

The plasma rifle's bolts had greater penetration than a laser

Plasma guns were slower than lasers and consumed more energy

Plasma bolts could penetrate even the most advanced armor

The plasma bolt punched through the soldier's armor

— USE GUN TAGS WITH FUTURISTIC WEAPONS —

Most of the modern gun tags can be used with futuristic energy and projectile weapons with minor modifications (swapping beams or bolts instead of bullets, battery packs instead ammo, and the sounds they make and damage they do). That's why there are fewer futuristic weapon tags, and why I've focused on more explanatory types of descriptions for them.

For added detail, create specific manufacturer and model numbers for your futuristic weapons, such as the "Zenergy Mark-5 Pulse-Ripper" or "Gravtek P-7 Plasma Rifle." You can then take this several steps further once you've introduced them by their full name to "Mark-5," "Pulse-Ripper," "P-7," or even nicknames, like "Fiver" or "PRip-gun." These make your weapons sound more real.

Monomolecular (also see Blades, Whips)

The mono-blade was half as durable as a sword but twice as deadly

The specially infused M-blade glowed red

The M-blade chopped through the plastic steam pipes

The armor-chewing V-sword vibrated 2,000 times a minute

The shredder's microscopically serrated edge sliced him in half

The whip handle housed a retractable 4-meter long monofilament wire

The mono-whip's wire could cut through flesh and most plastics

---

— WHAT ARE MONOMOLECULAR WEAPONS? —

A monomolecular weapon (also known as a mono- or "M" weapon) is made of a sole strand of tightly bonded carbon nanotubes or other moloecules. It will easily slice through flesh, glass, and metal while leaving other substances unharmed. The downside to monomolecular weapons is they are only half as durable as their normal counterparts and useless against plastic and other materials. Since most many futuristic armors incorporate plastic into their design, M-weapons are mostly employed by assassins, criminals, and mercenaries against civilian targets. (For the best example of an M-whip in action, read/watch *Johnny Mnemonic*.)

To create a monomolecular blade, the molecules are bonded to the weapon's edge. This means it never needs sharpening, although the rest of the weapon is subject to normal wear and tear. Some M-weapons are infused with a single color to give them a signature look, much like the colored lightsabers in *Star Wars*.

Battery-operated vibro-blades (also known as "shredders" or power- or "V" blades) are further enhanced to vibrate at 2,000 times a minute, thus giving them the properties of both a monomolecular weapon *and* a chainsaw. Unlike other M-weapons, V-blades emit a distinct hum when the battery is engaged.

Monofilament wire (sometimes called microfilament) has the same properties and is used to construct lethal nets and whips. The wielder of such a weapon must wear plastic gloves or gauntlets to catch, touch, or throw such weapons. M-whips are usually stored inside plastic gauntlets and pulled out when needed, with the added bonus that they can be retracted with the push of button.

The mono-whip sliced through flesh and bone

The weird whip cracked and hummed

The M-whip glowed red against the pale autumn night

The M-whip was used to garotte, grapple, or cut targets

The M-whip cracked, cutting the man in two

The M-whip wrapped around his neck, then ripped off his head

The web-gun fired a monofilament mesh net

The M-net closed over him, cutting and constricting

Caught in the closing web, the man was cut to pieces

Projectiles (also see Tranquilizer Guns)

One arm of the combat boomerang was cut short and sharpened to kill

The combat boomerang was not designed to return to its thrower

The combat boomerang split the man's head open and stuck in his skull

The needle-gun shot flechette rounds, often poison- or drug-tipped

A flechette rifle was also known as a needler or "sliver gun"

The sliver gun was like a near-silent shotgun loaded with lethal needles

Bio-guns fired flechette rounds to deliver disease to enemy troops

Their airguns fired paintballs filled with acid globes, drugs, or poison

The tangler shot a polymer capsule that quickly expanded into a net

The web-gun's polymer tendrils were almost unbreakable

The tangler's polymer net self-dissolved in twenty minutes

The pneumatic bolt gun shot armor-piercing spikes

The gun was made of glass and designed to squirt burning acid

Security Systems

Machine-guns popped down through ports in the ceiling

The drop-down machine-gun swiveled in our direction

A laser grid moved down the hall, slicing through anything it touched

The exits sealed as gas issued from jets mounted in the room's ceiling

A pit trap opened up under our feet, sending us sliding into darkness

The walls sprouted spikes and began to close in

Sonic

Infrasound created hallucinations and unease in the crowd

Ultrasound poured from the Nauseator cannons

The device quickly produced headaches and nausea in the target

The stunner pierced his ears, then his brain

Sonic weapons were often called "screamers"

The sonic pistol produced a sound that liquified organs and bone

The high-pitched whine of sonic weapons sent the crowd running

Dizziness, headache, and nausea overwhelmed the protestors

Spring-loaded (also see Blades)

The spring-loaded knife shot from the punk's forearm bracer

Claws sprang from his gauntlets

With a flick of his wrist, the battle gauntlet's blade extended

His wrist stump had been outfitted with a poisoned switchblade

— Guns —

Aiming and Firing

He aimed with speed and precision

The all-knowing eye of the gun peered into his soul

The dark circle of the muzzle commanded his attention

The gun's gaping eye bored into him

The barrel of his gun was a hungry cyclops

He sighted on screaming lips

He clenched his left eye shut and peered through the scope

The scope picked out the details of the target

His gun tracked the target, sighting in on the kill

Finger tensing on the trigger, he made the range at twenty yards

His crosshairs never left the target

His weapon never wavered

He watched her through the sniper scope

He drew a bead on his target

He took careful aim, knowing every shot had to count

She was caught in his sights

She took careful aim before pulling the trigger

He sighted along the barrel, picking his shot

A red laser eye of death blinked open on his chest

He stared down in horror as his chest lit up with little red lasers

Through his scope, the hidden sniper saw everything she did

He had the target in his sights

He eased the safety off and braced himself to get a better shot

He thumbed the safety off and steadied his aim

The bastard leveled the muzzle of his gun against the child's head

He squeezed two quick shots through shattered glass

He snapped off another round just to make sure

His answering fire was high and wide

He launched another flesh-mangling round

He took them both in rapid fire

He squeezed off a careful shot and ducked back

One flick of the trigger finished it

She caressed the trigger

Her finger found the trigger and tensed

Four times his trigger finger tightened, blasting lead

He snarled as he pulled the trigger

His finger curled around the trigger

His finger grew tight on the trigger, tense for killing

He popped off a quick shot before ducking behind cover

He dodged and weaved, shooting blind

He closed the gap between them with one pull of the trigger

He rattled off three shots in rapid order

He flung the car door open and came out firing

His trigger finger stroked familiar metal

Screaming death shot from the metal eye like tears of lead

Ammunition and Loading

The trigger clicked on empty

The firing chamber clacked open on empty

The magazine emptied in under two seconds

The firing bolt locked open on an empty chamber

The spent shells ejected in a clattering steel rain

Spent shell casings twirled around his head

She dropped the useless magazine and snugged the replacement in

He fed a fresh magazine into the hungry gun

He ejected the spent magazine and slammed in a spare

He fumbled a fresh magazine into the clip

He snapped a new magazine into the receiver and pulled back the bolt

He quickly chambered another round, knowing time was running out

He fed fresh death to the revolver with a speed-loader

He punched in a new clip and chambered a round

He quickly chambered another round

He slapped in another clip

He cursed and clawed for a full clip

His frantic fingers searched for a fresh clip

He plugged a long banana clip into the assault rifle

He fed the gun a fresh clip

> — FUTURISTIC TARGETING SYSTEMS —
> Most cyborgs, drones, robots, security systems, and smart weapons will have camera or computer-aided targeting to increase accuracy.

Automatic Weapons

The full-auto spoke death, and bullets were its words

He peppered the bodies with another deadly spray from his SMG

The old man's body jerked with the impact of each shot

The trio of 9mm flesh-rippers tore and twisted him from his perch

Flesh and fiber shredded under the Uzi's wicked assault

The chattering AK-47 tried to start a conversation with his vital organs

The .30 caliber machine gun chattered blind

She shot enough lead to kill three of him and only missed once

His gun added to the chorus of death being sung all around him

He poured a half-dozen rounds into him for good measure

He cut loose with the SMG as soon as the sentry looked his way

His AK-47 began a from-the-hip scattering of 7.62mm gut-rippers

The SMG chattered until its thirty-round vocabulary was done

The gangster let loose with a burst from his submachine gun

He switched to full-auto

The weapon's angry voice warned off the soldiers' pursuit

The rag doll figure did a clumsy backward somersault

Machine guns mulched flesh, mowing men down

Caught by the assault rifle's burst, the man did a jerky sidestep

The deadly drumming impact released a crimson river from his coat

A final burst swept him off his feet and pitched him down the staircase

He ended in a twitching sprawl across the vehicle's front seat

Blazing steel marched across the car hood in a relentless line

A gunner sprang into his path, blazing him with an automatic carbine

He snapped off a final burst, then turned and ran

Downwind, the hollow men danced a bloody two-step to the gun's beat

The machine gun spoke in stuttering bursts

The chattering gun weaved a whining figure eight over the target

He pinned the guard to the wall with a deadly figure eight

He stroked off another burst from the highly-modified M-16

Bullets riddled virgin flesh in a shooting gallery of horror

The steel jackets riddled them, sweeping them into leaking piles of flesh

The bodies twitched and fell, springing holes as if by magic

The machine gun swept the porch free of attackers

Not caring who he killed, the man pulled the trigger in an aimless spray

His trigger finger stroked out a quick three-round burst

A spattering of lead raked his flank

He returned fire with his Uzi one-handed

Hot death from the big guns blistered the general's troops to bits

The automatic rifle came to life again, ready to chop him to pieces

He swung his Uzi toward his attacker

Uzi fire crashed and rattled

The killers tumbled lifelessly, their torsos turned to soup by the barrage

The burst was short and surgically precise

A dozen bullets ripped flesh and fabric into bloody tatters

A dozen rounds picked the man up and slammed him against the wall

The Uzi shuddered out its shivering rain of death

The SMG's bullets punched him into a useless sprawl

The stutter-gun sizzled shot after shot at the fleeing fugitives

A line of 9mm slugs stitched the madmen as they raced forward

The brutal burst had the men thrashing like fish out of water

The blast had them breathing crimson foam from mangled lungs

The AK-47 had the men eating dirt stained black by their running blood

The stutter of AK-47s filled the night

The burp-gun belched and stuttered

A string of hot steel manglers spilled open his guts

The gunner cut loose with a deadly barrage that ripped the night

A blistering hot steel rain ripped from the bunker

The machine gun chattered, shredding men to pulp

A curtain of .30 flesh-manglers came down on the stage of his flesh

The high-powered assault rifles peppered the bodies into bloody rags

Set to full-auto, the weapon made short work of the advancing enemy

Body Hits

The first slug tore a hole through his heart

The bullet crunched through his ribcage and slammed into the wall

The slug struck his rib a glancing blow

The slug holed him through the heart

The bullet drilled him in the spine with a shattering of bone

Another slug crashed into his breastbone, throwing him back

The fresh round cored out the center of his chest

A grapefruit-sized hole punched through his back

The bullet bored a third, bloody nipple above her heart

A trio of holes slammed into his chest

The hot lead shower sent the soldier sprawling backward

A red hole erupted like a miniature oil well from his shoulder

The shot sizzled through his unprotected midsection

The bullet plowed a trail of destruction through her bare midriff

The round pierced her right breast, just above the nipple

His belly exploded in gut-ripping pain

Her pregnant belly heaved, springing crimson holes

As she ran, bullets punched bloody holes between her shoulder blades

His arm went numb, flapping like a broken bird where the bullet hit

Three of the slugs ripped into his chest, exiting in a juicy spurt of red

A bullet clipped her thigh

The slugs came ripping in at waist level

A tremor gripped the dying flesh, then stopped forever

The shots stitched inky red stains across his shirt

Liquid rushed out through the ragged hole

The force of impact lifted him off his feet, misting red

Bullets punched holes in the dam of his flesh, releasing a crimson tide

He clutched at kneecaps that were no longer there

Guts spilled from leaking abdomens

Giggling, the maniac poked his fingers into his victim's bullet holes

The soldiers' guns shredded the civilian mob, scattering them

Lower backs were skewered open by sizzling lead tumblers

Blood sprayed and bones shattered like pretzels

Shot in the back, the newly-made corpse corkscrewed into the lake

Screaming people were cut down as they ran for their cars

The angry bullet became a metallic messenger of death

The steel-jacketed bit of death sliced through vital meat and bone

The deadly slug bored its way into the guy's life pump

Savaged red matter expanded from the opening

A wall of crimson spurted from the bullet's impact

A pair of dull thuds smacked into him, spinning his body sideways

The bullet passed through his lung with a meaty splat

Expanding lead met yielding flesh

The impact spun him like a top, dumping him facedown on the carpet

The deadly impact sent him crashing to the floor in a crumpled heap

The hollow-point mushroomed on impact, ripping flesh from bone

The target toppled in an awkward sprawl

The target sagged backward, gushing vital juices

The intruder fell back through the window in an acrid haze

Blood red eyes opened on his chest, blinking gore

The fat man's belly ballooned red as he hit the floor

The deadly impact sent him tumbling

He lurched sideways on impact, clawing for his holster

He took a hit and dropped out of sight

The bullet crunched home

The bullet drove him back

He dodged the first shot, but not the next

The gun barked, then bit him

His gun squeezed off a message only death could answer

Sharp, precision fire took the enemy down

The high-impact rounds knocked him down and out

The bullet shrapneled on impact with his ribs

The bullet thundered into his heart

He took a round in the chest and fell back, saved by his kevlar vest

The bullets burst heart and lungs in a spattering of sticky red

Gunfights

The firefight blazed hot lead through the bitter night

The bullets buzzed like angry hornets around his head

Men burst from the building with guns blazing

Outside the house, gunfire raged

He hit the floor in a hail of bullets

Everyone who entered the kill zone ate a bullet

The renewed gunfire sparked a savage flurry of movement

The gunfire halted abruptly

A dozen figures cut through the brush, guns blazing

A storm of gunfire erupted, fast and fierce

Shots rang out on both sides, and soon, they were everywhere

A dozen guns opened up on each side, whizzing and whining death

Fierce and deadly, the firefight raged

It was all struggle, all hell—a flashing, blinding, chaos

Men scrambled for cover in the sudden chaos

The night was a smoking nightmare of screams and muzzle flashes

The first reports rolled in like distant thunder

Automatic weapons chattered in the distance

The gangsters flew out of their vehicles, guns blazing

Head Shots

A hole in its head, the torn body crumpled sideways

The steel-jacketed slug ripped him a new ear-hole

The first slug shredded the trachea just at the hollow of her throat

The second death-dealer plowed through the right frontal lobe

The 9mm burst walked up his torso and took him between the eyes

A chunk of bone the size of a child's fist exited the back of his skull

The slug slammed through the center of the guy's throat in a sea of red

The steel-jacketed missile made a Hiroshima of the guy's head

The soldier's head recoiled from the impact

Flesh and brains erupted in a liquid halo

A headshot finished the job

He lost half his face in a frothing red geyser

He ate hot lead as his face exploded

The .44 decapitated the first man to come through the door

Gushing holes were stitched across his forehead

He put a mercy round between her panicked eyes

The headshot sent the creep to an early dirt nap

Her face disintegrated with one pull of my trigger

He went down twitching, his skull ventilated

Like a ripe melon, his skull erupted

He put a point-blank penetrator though the skull

The skull-buster bounced his head back, spraying gore and gray matter

The 9mm punched through the tanned cheek, just under his left eye

The bullet exited her skull in a murky sea of crimson

His ruptured jugular dumped blood all over the carpet

A keyhole opened in his forehead, the lock turned explosively

His cap was blown away by a hot steel breeze, taking his scalp with it

The hat flew off, his scalp still inside

Heads burst like ripe fruit under that withering hail

The hat came off, and the top of his skull came with it

His white captain's hat shot off in a scarlet splatter

The bullseye dumped blood and brains down the front of his face

He laid a funeral wreath of hot lead across the bastard's face

The 9mm head-stopper blew his brains out in a crimson froth

The driver's head snapped back, his face dissolving in a crimson mask

Hot lead took his head off in a greasy shower of gore

Vicious hollow-points mushroomed inside his skull

The bullet smashed through the bridge of his nose, pulping brain

A fist-sized hole punched out the back of his skull

The shot girl gargled lead, spitting teeth

Raped by bullets, her once-beautiful face became a raw, dripping ruin

The bullet blazed through bone, spattering brains in a crimson mist

His skull exploded from the eyebrows up, vaporizing brain and bone

The heavy slug hit under his chin, vaporizing arteries in a pulsing mess

The lifeless girl collided with the wall and went down, oozing red

Headless human bowling pins toppled like cows to the slaughter

The 240-grain hollow-point shaved the lower jaw right off his face

A hollow-point hammered her head open like a hardboiled egg

Misses

Bullets chipped the pavement around him

A bullet whispered past his ear in a high-pitched whine

The stray slug took out a jagged section of windshield

Bullets ate the steps all around him

Bullets blasted the stained glass window, spraying colored shards

The Cadillac's windshield misted over with a spiderweb design

Floor tiles exploded as the intruder dumped his entire magazine at him

Armor-piercing rounds punched through their protection

The man next to me gargled lead, but I knew the shot was meant for me

He threw himself clear as bullets walked up the hood of the car

Lost, the bullet cried out for missing flesh

The target stepped out of sight just a second too soon

Suddenly, the curtains pulled shut and the sniper had no shot

Heavy slugs turned the windshield into cracked crystal

A bullet whistled past his ear

Hostile rounds were coming closer

He howled in terror as slugs whined off tree bark over his head

Screaming slugs slammed into the space he'd occupied seconds before

The shot went wide as he ran for cover

The bullet hit the chair where his head had been

More missed shots ripped and tore the air

A swarm of bullets buzzed over him like angry wasps

The line of slugs marched up the wall, narrowly missing him

Muzzle Flashes

The weapon's muzzle flashed white-hot in the distance

A tongue of flame announced the bullet's birth

Cones of fire blossomed from their rifles in controlled bursts

The yellow flash of muzzle blasts were visible forty yards away

Return fire flashed at him

Muzzle flashes ripped the night like deadly dragons

Yellow fire flashed from the treeline

He aimed at the muzzle flashes, hoping for a kill

A blaze of fiery light pinpointed the gunman

Muzzle flashes illuminated the two gunmen in the doorway

Yellow-orange light strobed the room

The muzzle flashes revealed their cruel faces with executioner's eyes

A sudden flash of fire picked out a lone gunman in the distance

Flame stabbed from the big gun's muzzle

Yellow daggers of flame popped from the barrels as they shot

Muzzle flashes stabbed the darkness

Pistols

The blast from the .45 ground into his gut, giving him a second navel

The .38 caliber killer tunneled into his groin with a sickening *thud*

The big .45 barked death

Pistol extended like a second fist, he stepped bravely into the room

He used both hands to steady the big .45

He triggered a 9mm probe in the night

The crack of the pistol put an end to him once and for all

Sparks flashed from the soldier's .45

The .45 flapped from its holster, spitting death

The heavy reports of the .45 thundered through the night

The .45 heart-stopper did its job

The silver handgun's booming thunder took the men down

Her ears objected to the rolling thunder of the big weapon

The 9mm manglers dropped the mob into a thrashing, screaming mass

He swung the .357 around to find his next target

He squeezed a shot through the glass, seeking flesh

Lunging sideways, the detective clawed for his shoulder holster

The cop reached inside his coat for the .38

The officer's hand reached for a holstered sidearm

A huge handgun boomed, barking death

He dropped the still-smoking revolver and raised his hands

The cold muzzle of the .44 Magnum rested against his skull

Satisfied, he thrust the pistol into his belt

The killer pumped lead at him from a semiautomatic

The hand cannon boomed in his fist

The .357's blast blew him away like a rag in high wind

She reversed the weapon and clubbed her victim across the face

He slashed the suspect across the face with his pistol, laying the cheek open to the bone

The butt of the gun bounced off his skull, sending him into darkness

Calmly, the man raised the pistol to his temple and pulled the trigger

He ate the barrel of his gun and pulled the trigger

Rifles

The rifleman tensed, waiting

He snapped the rifle up, seeking targets

Rifle shots cracked in the distance

They held their empty rifles like clubs

The riflemen advanced, bayonets at the ready

He set his bayonet for the charge

He slammed the bolt home and squeezed the trigger

The bolt-action rifle was old, but still knew how to kill

The hunting rifle would shoot him a new kind of meat—the human kind

Metal glinted in the sunlight a second before the rifle shot rang out

He eased the door open with the business end of his rifle

The muskets roared, booming balls of death toward the enemy line

From the ridge, a range-rider sniped at him

A rifle bullet burned along his ribs

The rifle round ripped through the air

The rifle roared in his hands

Rifle rounds *pinged* and whined off the rocks

He caved in her teeth with the rifle butt

He slung the rifle over his shoulder in relief

The rifle stock kicked against his shoulder

The rifle ripped him a new one

The rifle felt good against shoulder

Silencers

The silencer coughed against the pillow

He eased the silenced Beretta from its leather holster

The silenced pistol blew deadly kisses at her command

The silencer whispered once into his ear

Twice, the assassin's pistol coughed, and twice, men died

The sound-suppressed weapon whispered the secret names of death

The silenced weapon gave no distinctive muzzle flash or deadly bark

A ruthless weapon, it did its job quietly and efficiently–just like him

The silencer kissed her goodnight

There was a deadly *phut*, then the smell of gun smoke

The assassin unscrewed the silencer and pocketed it

The killer wrapped the gun's barrel with his silencer

The silenced pistol pulled him forward through the rooms like a magnet

Shotguns

The shotgun round *chunked* the cowboy's flesh to gravy

His shotgun boomed, blasting the door open

The boom-stick belched smoke and fire

A sudden lick of flame came from the shotgun

The shotgun spit double-barreled death

He brandished the empty shotgun like a club

The shotgun blast ripped through the door

He dumped shells into his pockets

He pumped the shotgun once

The shotgun pump *ka-chakked* in his hands

He extended the shotgun through the open door, ready for anything

With one pull, the shotgun solved what years of therapy couldn't fix

He swung the riot gun up, hoping for an easy kill

A charge of buckshot took him chest-high and lifted him off his feet

Buckshot peppered the intruder's backside as he made a run for it

The shotgunner saw him coming and readied a blast

The sawed-off shotgun made his head disappear like a magic trick

He scooped up the shotgun, ready for action

A shotgun roared, its pellets raking red revenge on the ruined face

The sawed-off shotgun thundered in his fist

The sawed-off barrel made short work of the intruder

He braced the shotgun under his chin and pulled the trigger

The shotgun blast decorated the wall a savage red

The combat shotgun sheared flesh from bone, pulping internal organs

The shotgun punched holes through people and walls

He took a shotgun blast to the face and died instantly

The roaring shotgun tore bodies like tissue paper

Tranquilizer Guns

He loaded a dart in the tranq gun and prayed it would be enough

The tranquilizer gun coughed

The dart went deep into my shoulder

I could not reach the dart in my back no matter how hard I tried

I stared at the dart sprouting from my chest in disbelief

The dart sprang from my chest as if by magic

They pumped me full of enough tranquilizer to knock out an elephant

Yanking the dart from his arm, he staggered and swayed to the door

The venom-coated dart shot into the man's back

The feathered dart sank in and sleep soon followed

The tufted dart was a ballistic syringe

The darts were filled with a sleep agent

The darts were filled with a paralytic agent

The darts were filled with a biological agent

The darts were filled with deadly poison

— WHAT TYPE OF GUN IS IT? —

Technology constantly evolves, so I've kept the various gun tags as generic as possible. Feel free to insert your favorite guns instead.

Impalement

Bows and Crossbows

His life ended with one twang of my bow

He drew back the bow and took careful aim at his target

The arrow took her in the knee and she crumpled to the ground

He broke the shaft off and pulled the rest of the arrow clean through

The arrow took her in the arm, pinning her to the tree

One creak of the wood, one twang of the string, and it went flying

Everything with the bow had to be one shot, one kill

It was hunting season all over again—only this prey walked on two legs

Dumbstruck, he stared at the feathered shaft protruding from his chest

He pulled back his bow and the sky rained death

No arrow was faster, no kill cleaner than by his hand

A feathered shaft sprouted from his eye as if by some dark magic

Taken through the neck, the sentry toppled silently over the wall

He had been impaled on a forest of arrows, yet still clung feebly to life

An arrow through the heart ended her love

Bow in hand, he stalked through the long, dark woods

By the time the archer was through, the man was a human pincushion

The arrows screamed and the sky grew black with death

A rain of arrows fell upon their heads

There was that awful *twang* before the arrow found him

A snapped bowstring was the least of his worries

Whizzing, screaming death flew in those feathered shafts

The whiz and *twang* of the bow brought death

The well-arrowed corpse tumbled from the wall into the waiting moat

The shaft stuck out of him like an exclamation point

The arrow's fletching was unmistakably eagle's feather

The arrows flew overhead, thick as thieves in the night

Arrows fell in a cold steel rain

The archer's quiver was nearly exhausted

He planted arrows in the dirt in a semicircle, so they'd be ready to fire

The bolt struck the man in the chest and he went down gasping

The crossbow strummed its deadly chord

A bolt shot him through the heart

The drawstring hummed, spitting death

He pulled back the heavy drawstring and slid the bolt into place

She watched her prey through the scope of her crossbow

Crossbow clutched firmly to her breast, she vowed courage

She pulled the trigger and watched the bolt strike him dead

The bullet-headed bolt bit into his neck

A barbed bolt transfixed him

She raised the crossbow pistol and aimed for his chest

His finger convulsed on the trigger, driving the bolt home

He grabbed a bolt to reload

The crossbow bolt skimmed by, startling him

Her shot spiked him to the tree

Spears, Spikes, and Pointy Things

The spear skewered him to the wall with a meaty *thunk*

He used the spear as leverage to force his opponent back

He whittled the long branch into a makeshift spear

He threw the makeshift spear with all his might

The diamond-shaped head lanced through him

The spear penetrated her as deeply as any lover

The spear ripped out, revealing a bloody perforation of meat and organs

The spear stabbed him, lifting him up and over the madman's head

The stabbing pain of the spear in his side crippled him

Too late, he grabbed at the shaft

The spear spiked him to the wall

His savaged body slumped down the spear's shaft

The pierced heart pumped its last as I turned the spear and twisted

The javelin pinned her to the ground and would not let her go

He used the rifle like a spear, thrusting the bayonet forward

The rifle's bayonet speared the intruder back out the cabin door

The knight's lance slammed him off his mount and into the dirt

The harpoon took him through the chest and he clawed feebly at it

The trident's barbed prongs thrust forward

The pitchfork punched through him as easily as a fork at the salad bar

The pitchfork pinned him to the barn wall

The pitchfork punished him with a cold steel punch

He fell from the hayloft onto the angry pitchforks below

The pitchfork's ghoulish prongs slid into her belly like fangs

Betrayed by gravity, the victim's body slid down the impaling spike

He landed on the wrought iron spikes below and hung there, helpless

The metal spike crunched into his gut and came out the other side

The spiked portcullis dropped down, pinning him to the castle floor

The killer staggered back under the weight and impact of the weapon

The pickaxe pierced his chest like the fang of some monstrous spider

The pickaxe dug for buried treasure in the victim's brain

The beast's horns gored his flesh, throwing him like a wet rag

The taxidermist lunged at me with a ragged piece of antler

A knitting needle stabbed his throat, sewing shut the gates of life

The tent spike made an excellent improvised weapon

She hammered the spike home in his flesh

He used the sharp end of the broken branch to skewer the brute's chest

The broken tree branch punched through his lung

The fishing gaff's barbed hook dug into her belly, yanking her back

The meathook tore into the naked meat of her thigh

A meathook grabbed his shoulder, dragging him to the slaughter

Gristle dripped from the bloody hook

The maniac had a hook for a hand and wasn't afraid to use it

The madman swung his silver hook at him

— KILLERS WITH UNUSUAL WEAPONS —

Odd weapons can make your killer stand out. Some slasher movie examples: *The Burning* (hedge clippers), *My Bloody Valentine* (pickaxe), *The Mutilator* (fishing gaff), *The Prowler* (pitchfork).

LIQUIDS and VAPORS

Acid

A thin film ate away at his face until nothing was left

It burned her skin in an unholy agony of raw, liquid fire

She was lowered into an acid vat where no beauty could remain

The acid crawled across her face and into her eyes

It ate its way into her until she thought she would die

Acid-scorched skin gave way to bleached bone

A grisly burning was on her skin, in her eyes, nose, and throat

One splash burned her beauty into ugliness

The acid ate away everything that made him human

The acid dissolved his body, boiling it into smoking mush

Fizzing, hissing death consumed him

It was a chemical peel from hell

His twisted, acid-scarred face was a thing born out of nightmare

The mask hid an acid-scarred face melted by hate

Melted flesh and bubbling bone were all that remained

The acid destroyed any outward appearance of his humanity

The foul, chemical soup consumed her

His bones floated in the glass tank, then they too were gone

Wherever the acid touched, pain blazed

His flesh became a melted ruin in that steaming soup

The foul-smelling bath bleached flesh from bone

Jackson Dean Chase

Drowning

As the lake's glassy waters closed over his head, he stared up her

Water filled her lungs

She thrashed desperately toward the surface

Cruel fingers held her head underwater

He watched the bubbles burst from between her ruby lips

Nature's cruel current carried her far from shore

Far from the safety of the pier, death washed over her

The tide took her

Gripped by thoughts of suicide, he rowed out to the center of the lake

The shore seemed very far away as his strength failed

The current claimed her

Saltwater choked her lungs, making her gag

Churning waves pulled him from my grasp, and then I saw him no more

Chained to the cement block, he held his breath as long as he could

The chill blue waters filled her lungs and emptied her of life

The numbing waters washed over him in their icy-blue embrace

The sea seemed a peaceful way to go til he couldn't breathe

The ocean ended him in a cold splash of death

She kicked and gurgled, clawing for air as the killer held her down

He opened his mouth and cried for help, but only seagulls answered

Choking, salty death poured into his burning lungs

The watery grave shrouded her in its liquid coffin

The sucking swamp buried her in its murky waters

She vanished without a trace beneath the lake's surface

The shore seemed far away and unimportant to the drowning man

Gasping for air, her head broke the surface as she flailed for help

He thrashed and screamed as the quicksand claimed him

He knew her drowned body would be food for snakes and gators and all the crawling things that hid in the swamp

Soon, even his hands sank out of sight

Poison and Gassing

There was a bitter taste of almonds, then nothing more

Gasping, gurgling, she fell back against her chair

Through foam-flecked lips, she writhed and moaned

The poison ate away at his guts

He gagged as his hands flew to his throat

He drank the strange cocktail and seconds later, he was dead

Poison coursed through his veins, burning him from the inside

The first, faint blush of death blossomed on her cheeks

Her eyes grew wide as her breath grew short

He mixed her drink with a knowing smile

Once stirred into the drink, the drug dissolved effortlessly

With a desperate sob, she poured the pills down her throat

The poison left no trace

The bluish tinge to his lips was a sure sign of poison

He choked and his breath came in ragged gasps

His breathing became labored, his footsteps unsteady

The pills had been ground to a fine powder, perfect for poison

She drank her death with a knowing smile

She gobbled pills, dozens of them, and prayed for death to find her

The cruel needle injected the killer liquid into the man's body

The toxic fumes burned like fire in her lungs

The gas stripped the flesh from his throat and lungs

The strangling fumes left him voiceless in his final moments

There was a strange smell, a sinister haze, and then it was too late

The room was quiet except for the steady hiss of the gas

A vapor from hell reeked and ravaged, leaving lifeless bodies in its wake

The smell was the first thing he noticed . . . and the last

Every gasp was torture, every moment terror

The fumes robbed her of her senses, sent her tumbling to the floor

Under the spell of those sinister fumes, she slept

A cloud of deadly gas blew from the pipes

The vapor burned and strangled, choked, and killed

With the hissing of the gas, blackness descended on him

There was no air left that was not tainted

He fell into the fumes' midnight embrace

The mustard gas made short work of his eyes, nose, throat, and lungs

He could not breathe, only claw at his throat

In an instant, thick, choking clouds of tear gas rolled out to meet him

The nerve gas had his whole body shaking like a leaf in the wind

The nerve gas sent him writhing to the ground in twitching agony

STRANGULATION

Hanging and Neck Snaps

The gallows noose tightened around his neck

The trapdoor snapped open, sending the doomed man to his death

They laughed as the hanged man kicked and jerked in the still night air

The branches of the Hanging Tree bore the bitter fruit of our dead

The Hanging Tree's branches were heavy with human fruit

The noose tightened around his neck

With bulging eyes and lolling tongue, the hanged man's face purpled

The men heaved and the killer rope dragged him off his feet

The deadly rope broke his neck on impact

The rope failed to break his neck, leaving him to kick and strangle

The noose tightened, the chair clattered, and he died

Soon there was only the sound of the rope creaking its strange, sad tune

He twisted her head at an impossible angle, snapping her frail neck

Inhumanly strong hands clutched his neck, twisting, twisting . . .

The boy's neck broke like a rotten branch

He yanked and twisted until the bones popped and life left

There was a gruesome snap, then her head rolled at a crazy angle

The man's neck bones grated and snapped

The head flopped forward on its broken neck

He snapped her neck like a dry twig

The neck broke with a grinding crunch

Strangling by Device

The piano wire took his air, then sliced clean through his throat

With a wire garrotte held between both hands, he crept forward

He slipped the piano wire over the guy's head

He tightened his muscles to make the wire cut quick and deep

The thin, unbreakable wire sliced through the man's throat

He clawed at the savage wire, gasping for air

The killer wire cut deep, vanishing into the flesh of his throat

He pulled the grisly wire back from the nearly-severed head

He wiped the bloody wire clean on the man's immaculate suit

Wound tight by powerful hands, the barbed wire sank into her throat

The barbed wire bit into her neck

The cord wound tightly, pulling him backward into death

He yanked back on the electrical cord with savage fury

He wound the rope tightly around both hands and snapped it taut

The savage rope left a deep purple bruise around her pretty neck

The necktie was a perfect fit for his victim's swan-like throat

---

— Important Strangling Details —

Unlike the movies, people being strangled in real life *do not* make a lot of noise. There is the initial gasp and gurgle, then they go silent because no air passing through the throat equals no noise—except maybe a few muted ones as the killer loosens and adjusts his grip to get more comfortable (and deadly). As the strangling continues, the victim's mouth will gape wide, lusting for air, and the tongue will protrude, often remaining somewhat past the lips after death.

    It can take several minutes for a strangling victim to die. Again, this is where the movies get it wrong, condensing what should be a major event into impossibly brief seconds.

The necktie became a makeshift noose in his hands

The stocking stretched tight across her throat

Her eyes bulged and mouth gasped as the stocking grew still tighter

The nylon formed a black line through which no air could pass

The nylon whispered sweet death around her throat

Desperate, he strangled her with her own pantyhose

She pulled the nylon tight around his neck

Strangling by Hands

Air was everywhere except in his lungs

His mouth cried out for it, yet no sound would come

His face purpled under the relentless assault

His eyes bulged and her tongue swelled, thirsty for air

His fingers found her throat and squeezed until she was no more

Heavy, crushing hands closed about her neck

Through reddened face and bulging eyes, her mouth made its last gasping "O" of life

Powerful hands cruelly caressed her ivory throat

The choking hands squeezed until she could breathe no more

Unlike the movies, the girl made no sound except the odd gurgle

He strangled her life away

Her struggles subsided as the air ran out

He lifted her off her feet, his powerful hands crushing her throat

Between bulging eyes and purpled throat, her tongue poked past the corner of her mouth

The tongue dangling from her strangled face was a dainty pink reminder of the pleasure she'd given only hours before

His body tensed in one final contortion

His twisted mouth struggled to draw oxygen in

His thumbs dug into her throat, squeezing off the supply of air

The eyes glazed and hands drooped as all air left her lungs

The air rushed out of him under that ruthless grip

Thumbs dug into his windpipe

The tyranny of his fingers bore down on his neck

The cop's chokehold sent him spinning into darkness

He choked her out, then carried the limp body to the trunk of his car

Head lolling, mouth dripping saliva, she surrendered to his strength

His eyes nearly popped out of his head as he struggled for breath

His mouth slacked open, strings of saliva rolling down his chin

Black spots danced in his eyes as he struggled for breath

— WRITING EFFECTIVE ACTION SCENES —

To write effective action, don't go into more detail than you have to, and don't let your characters pause to reflect on what is happening. Would you have time to think or say more than a few words in a real fight? No! Short sentences and short paragraphs ratchet up pacing and suspense. Like when our hero confronts gang-bangers:

Snake Samson drew his Desert Eagle. The big gun blew death into the closest street scum. Bodies hit the wall, gushing life. Screaming. Sobbing. Dying.

The remaining gang-bangers panicked. Some ran. Others dove for cover. And the rest opened fire . . .

—Wounds and Corpses —

Blood and Gore

The first scarlet drops flowed like ghastly flowers blooming in the night

Choking on his own blood, he staggered back in disbelief

A crimson rain burst from his chest

Her blood was a scarlet river flowing on waves of pain

Pulsing arteries pumped their last

The shotgunned ceiling wept red tears

The leaking fluids went *drip-drip-drip*

The life force gushed out of him

Her hand came away from her face sticky and red with the juices of life

Crimson bubbles burst past gore-caked lips

An awful cry sprang from his throat as the gore gushed out

He gargled on gore, spitting bloody froth and phlegm

The blood flowed, the children screamed, and the horror began

She was wet with gore, glistening in the moonlight

He was crowned in crimson

He bled out, the stink of copper his only companion

Blood flowered from her wound in crimson petals

The trail of gore led to a red room washed in death

She pressed tighter the wound, trying to staunch the sticky red flow

Blood was the lubrication of life, but also death, and he gloried in it

He gloried in gore, making handprints and scribbling insane messages

The fluids spilled out of her so fast she nearly slipped on her blood

As the last drops of life left him, he thought of her and smiled

Wet-hot drops of crimson splattered the upturned faces of the crowd

Greasy with gore, the killer slipped and slid in the blood and excrement

The taste of copper was in his mouth now

His face was a death mask, dripping red with blood, hot with hate

In her bloody smile was the acceptance of death

Liquid rubies rained from the wound like ghastly treasure

Blood covered her naked body in a crimson dress

Shrouded in gore, a red mist danced before his eyes

The ragged wound wept tears of blood

Rivulets of blood ran down his screaming face

Blood burst in foaming bubbles from his mouth

Hot, bubbling gore showered the crowd

A red rain drifted down

Her blood was all over him

The blood of the innocent bathed him, washing his sins

A shroud of crimson gore wrapped her in death

Drooling blood, he staggered back in disbelief

Bleeding out, he took two steps to his right and fell down the stairs

A fountain of fatal red pulsed from the wound

The lethal wound spurted crimson death

The hole was a fast-flowing sea of fatal red

A pillar of gushing life shot up from the wound, painting the ceiling

Hot, gushing horror swam across the floor, red and relentless

Blood spilled from the wound

Bloody spittle drooled from his foaming mouth in scarlet threads

Blood geysered from the ragged wound

Blood blew from him in a sticky fountain

Crimson fire burned out of the wound in hot, gushing spurts

Gore-caked fingers probed red, crusting lips

Blood caked and congealed into crusty scabs across his skin

The blood showered off her broken body like scarlet rain

He was sick, sticky with his own blood, and vomiting

His guilt and her gore wrapped him like a shroud

Gore-crusted lips muttered feeble prayers to an uncaring god

An incredible quantity of blood poured from the hole in her breast

His white shirt was crimson by the time I got to him

Blood welled up and began to flow

He had lost a lot of blood and was losing more

He felt faint from loss of blood, but struggled on

The carnage was complete

Dead Bodies

A bloody hand clawed out of the pile of butchered bodies, clawing at air

All around were the dead and dying, blood-spattered and broken

A gore-caked corpse congealed in the corner

Blood-smeared and shabby, the corpse was clad in old rags

The shriveled remains were as forgotten as the victim's name

That there were no visible wounds made the death more suspicious

A ragged hole in the dead man's neck left no doubt as to cause of death

The frozen bodies were stacked like cordwood

The corpse was a blasted husk in which no trace of soul remained

From the look of terror etched on that awful face, I had no desire to share his fate

The stench of the dead man's loosening bowels hit me in the face

The corpse as if she had jumped into death's arms willingly

The bodies lay blackened and burned to ash

The corpses were grim reminders of what might have been

The basement was a cobwebbed horror of stacked bodies and secret hell

The dead girl's flesh was alive with maggots

Worms crawled over her lips like lovers

A lone gray worm wiggled its way from the dead man's nose

The girl was long dead, her body ripe with rot

Her body was pregnant with the putrescence of death

The dead man hit the ground with a sickening thud

Of the original victims, only the heads remained

Their bodies were propped, as if in prayer

His blood was still, his heart stopped

He had died as he had lived

A soul-blasted corpse regarded him with unseeing eyes

The grisly remains bore mute witness to the horror she now faced

The body was rife with corruption

Without limbs or head to match, the torso was unidentifiable

A maniac had stitched the bodies together in a mismatched patchwork

The corpse glared at me, daring me to not to join it

They were discarded mannequins, silent and immobile

Inspecting the bodies, nearly every kill was a head shot

The butchery was indescribable

The bodies no longer resembled anything human

The skeleton leered at her from its hiding place

The dry heat had mummified the body rather than decomposed it

They dredged the bloated body out of the lake

The body washed ashore two days later, a bloated nightmare

The fish had eaten away the eyes and most of the face

The crabs had clawed away most of the face-meat

The body lay in the field, stinking of opened guts and empty promises

A scalpel had razored her bloodless lips into a grin wider than life

The corpse's face had frozen in a terrified scream

The mouth was impossibly wide and horrible in that shriveled face

The gory remains greeted me as I walked in the door

Buzzing flies hung like a halo over the corpse's head

Flies crawled on the congealed ruin of her mangled body

The hollow-eyed corpse grinned back at me as if making a joke

A fat fly crawled over the corpse's ruined cheek, drinking blood

Hungry maggots oozed out of putrid flesh

Squirming minions of madness, the blind maggots ate

The crawling things of the earth covered her like a living blanket

Maggots feasted on the rotten remains

Plump, juicy maggots bore holes in him, drilling for the oil of death

The corpse in the coffin looked strangely at peace, considering . . .

The funeral was open casket, but I couldn't look

Even stretched out on the autopsy table, her beauty was undiminished

The coroner cut into the corpse, searching for secrets

Bodies in zippered black plastic were ushered into the ambulance

The paramedics hefted the body bag into the waiting ambulance

The body-filled morgue was cold and stank of antiseptic

The pathologist pulled the steel drawer open, revealing the victim

Dead or not, the unnatural state of the bodies unnerved me

In death, as in life, I could not face her

Bodies draped under sheets greeted me like old friends

The victim's remains lay on the autopsy table, ready for inspection

The corpse had the distinctive stitched "Y" of an autopsy scar

Decapitation and Head Trauma

The man's head disappeared in a red mist

Blood and brains burst out of his shattered skull

The mad doctor's drill tunneled into her skull

The back of his skull burst open like a ripe melon

He sputtered and puked as his brains leaked out

Zippers of blood ran down his forehead

The pink jam of pulped brain squished beneath his boot

Action Writers' Phrase Book

Skull sheared off, he staggered toward me, unaware he was dead

With a look of surprise, her severed head fell wetly to the floor

Her fingers squished into the red hole, massaging his exposed brain

His head flopped down onto his chest, hanging by a crimson string

One blow killed him and the second took his head clean off

Melted brain leaked out of the corpse like clumps of gray jam

He clutched at the mangled ruins of his face

Hair fluttering like wings, the head flew from her neck

Her severed head was a baby bird leaving the nest of her shoulders

His severed head stared at me until the last spark of life faded

His face was a crimson mask of horror, flesh peeled back to the bone

The brain was gone, scooped out like ice cream

As his mangled head tipped forward, the exposed brain plopped out

Frantic hands groped for his missing head, but found only crimson air

I watched in horror as what was left of his brain came sliding out

Her head would make a fine trophy, right next to the twelve-point buck

The head tumbled away from the spurting stump

The guillotine bit his neck and the bucket collected his head

The sword swung, the head rolled, and the curse was broken

Dribbling brains, the poor bastard gagged on his own vomit and died

The clockwork slicing of the pendulum blade carried his head clean off

The sword savaged his throat until his head came away from his neck

Slicing, severing death sang out and her head obeyed the call

He reached for his missing cranium and felt empty air

A fountain of red flowed from where his head had been

Dismemberment

The air was stained scarlet by his spurting stump

The jagged limb jerked, then lay still on the saw mill floor

He stared in horror at his severed hand

Still twitching, the mutilated member flopped to the floor

The killer took his arm off at the shoulder

The severed hand crawled away, possessed by a life of its own

Without legs, the creature fell

Robbed of her limbs, the amputated girl was helpless to resist

He clutched the gushing red stump as if to stop the flow with his fingers

The blood splashed in buckets from the severed stump of his arm

Blood painted the walls wherever the mangled stump was raised

The limb came off and hit the floor with a ragged plop

Her leg was sheared off just above the knee

The bone stuck out of the butchered arm like an accusing finger

Gore grew from her severed wrist like fingers of blood

The fingers flew and limbs fell

His chopped wrist squirted blood across her face

Blood pulsed in spurts from the ruined limb

What was left of his leg bled out like a butcher shop

The savaged stump was squirting blood like a fire hydrant from hell

The enraged ape ripped his arm off and beat him to death with it

Pulled apart, all he could do was die

Blood pulsed in waves from the severed wrist

The screaming stump raged red ruin

The hand came off at the wrist with a sickening crunch

His severed leg lay mangled next to him as he bled out in the corner

The first blow lopped off the front half of her pedicured foot

He kept madly trying to reattach the ripped hand to its bleeding stump

Ragged red lines squirted from his wetly-chopped wrist

Blood burst from the missing limb's socket in a relentless red rush

The arm tore free from the shoulder with a sickening wet crunch

He yanked on the dangling limb, twisting it free from its socket

Whistling a merry tune, he snipped off her fingers

Eye Injuries

Ragged strips of flesh clung to his cheeks below the missing eyes

She stared at me through two sightless holes where her eyes had been

His right eye hung limply against his cheek

His thumbs found the sockets and pressed hard

Frenzied fingers dug in until the eyes burst and the black fluid squished

The object pierced her eye before she could even scream

The hedge clippers cut through the blue of her eyes, then snapped shut

His eyes burst like two balloons, weeping black and red

Punctured and bleeding, his eye was a raw ruin that oozed down his cheek like a runny egg

His thumbs scooped into the sockets, smashing eyes to sightless jelly

His fingers dug into her eye socket and scooped out the gory prize

The ruined eye dripped to the floor

The missing eye rolled under the chair like a child's toy

The poker burned the hateful look from her eyes, but not the curses from her tongue

The scalpel took her eyes and everything else of independence

Blind, she clawed and moaned for him to save her

With no eyes to guide him, still he came toward her, grim and relentless

She spooned out his eyes and filled the juicy sockets with maggots

The hypodermic needle pierced the eye, squirting his brain with death

Blinded and alone, he waited to die

A barbecue fork pierced both eye and brain

A hot poker put out the prisoner's eyes, sizzling them shut forever

His eyes were like two scrambled eggs that oozed and dripped

With one last, awful squish, the eyes popped out of their sockets

The eyeball hung by a thin red string, flopping against her cheek

With crude stitches, the creep sewed her eyes shut, then everything else

Gutting

Disemboweled, he stumbled back as his entrails spilled out

Eviscerating her sounded classy compared to what he had done

He kneeled in pain, both hands clutching his open abdomen

His guts poured like wine onto the rough cement floor

Life drained through that terrible wound, the guts last of all

Her guts hung from the rafters like party streamers

Action Writers' Phrase Book

Blood shot from his mouth as reeking guts boiled over his crotch

Intestines leaked from him in a hopeless tangle of doom and death

He clutched frantically at the intestines uncoiling into his lap

Steaming ropes of blood-smeared intestines spilled through his fingers

The contents of her overripe belly slid onto the floor, the fetus last of all

One by one, the organs oozed out of her mangled stomach

The steaming offal oozed from her soft belly

Her belly was a raw wound that gave birth to wetly-plopping organs

His guts steamed and writhed like snakes in a sauna

His intestines squirmed and squished like hungry snakes

Her belly burst, giving birth to the scarlet children within

One stroke and his guts came out in a tangled web of horror

She choked on the stench of ripe intestines and broken bowels

The slippery ropes poured out as he tried to shove them back in

The first yellowish loops of intestine squirmed from the wound

His mutilated guts stank and steamed in his lap like giant worms

The blade gutted him like a fish

He reeled back, uncomprehending, as his organs leaked out

The first ghastly worm of intestine peered from the gaping hole

Blood and bile broke free from the wound—her guts were soon to follow

Frantic fingers clutched and clawed at her mutilated belly

She tried to hold back the inevitable doom of her leaking guts

He collapsed in a crumpled heap of mangled guts and gore

The madman strangled the woman with her own intestines

As his guts leaked out, he knew this was the end

Whips and Torture

She gave a whole new definition to the term, "cruel and unusual"

The sadistic woman chuckled softly, brandishing her whip

When it was done, he was a freak of flayed skin and missing face

The sting of the lash carried the weight of his authority

The whip welts were deep and hideous, rimmed with blood

The lash laid thin ragged lines of red into her tanned flesh

The brutal flogging left his back a dripping ruin

The whip stung her, peeling the soft flesh from her bones in cruel strips

Cruel barbs bit into her flesh as the cat o' nine tails caressed her back

Stinging, burning pain became the whole of his world

The lash drove screams from her throat she didn't know she had

The whips cracked like claws against the bloody ruin of her back

The lash was practically a comfort compared to this new horror

The ropes tightened, the whip cracked, and she begged for mercy

The whipping continued without respite or relief

She tried to hold his image in her mind, but the whip soon replaced it

---

— TORTURE DEVICES —

Some medieval devices have obvious, self-explanatory names, like the breast-ripper or dunking chair, while others are called by more poetic, religious, or humorous names—the Pear of Agony, Judas Cradle, and Spanish Tickler all come to mind.

Consider whether your torturer is a "purist" devoted to collecting and/or fabricating copies of authentic historical devices, or whether he wishes to invent and perfect his own even more terrible creation. Perhaps your villain looks down on the crude methods of the past and prefers modern techniques such as waterboarding.

The chains were cold against my skin

The manacles scraped and chafed

The handcuffs bit into cruelly into my wrists

The iron poker glowed red-hot against his skin

The torture continued, so that she must either break or go mad

Cold steel pliers pinched and pulled skin made tender by the lash

Hot tongs charred and bent my skin

The torture doctor experimented on her trapped and tender flesh

He locked her head inside a cage of hungry rats and watched the fun

A hammer and chisel made short work of his porcelain veneers

Teeth were pried out amid the crunching of bone

The toothless maw gaped at me, a blood-drooling mess

The prisoner was a broken, bleeding wreck, hopeless in his torment

The needle pinched, injecting agony

The needle went under the skin and came out the other side

When he saw the instruments of torture laid out, his will to resist broke

Nailed to the cross, her expression was anything but angelic

The broken man whispered his confession in my ear

The blood-mad fiend began his butcher's work

It was a controlled slaughter I witnessed on that torture table

The rough-hewn walls of the torture chamber ran red with blood

He sliced off her lying lips and fed them to his dog

The torturer's gaze was hollow, his eyes cruel and dead

The torturer's tone was cordial even during the worst

He was proud of his ghoulish profession

The air seemed heavy with the weight of a thousand screams

It was a sick game he played, one I was helpless to win

I closed my eyes and prayed for it to end

I shut my eyes against the ungodly pain

The torture ended in a blood-red splash of agony

The confession spilled from her as easily as her blood

At this point, he would confess to anything just make her stop

A jumble of truth and lies spilled from the tortured boy's tongue

Her castrating claws went to work, mangling his manhood

He rubbed salt into the wounds, wringing fresh agony from his victim

The victim's body was painted with honey for the flies to feast on

Hot wax dripped from the madman's candle over her shuddering flesh

He was buried up to his neck and left to be eaten by the animals

---

— INSIDE THE TORTURER'S TWISTED MIND —

Does your villain enjoy torturing his victims, or is it only a job to him—a necessary evil? Is he a hot-blooded sadist aroused by pain, or a cold fish lacking even the most basic emotion? Humans are complex creatures, and your villain should be no exception. Perhaps he tortures only those he feels "deserve" it, granting those he respects a quick, merciful death.

Does your villain love his wife and children? His pet cat? Is he kind to his neighbors and coworkers? Does he have other, more dignified hobbies, like composing poetry or growing roses?

The more you know about your villain and his motives, the more real you can make him to your reader. For example, a poetry-loving villain might draw "inspiration" from a certain victim, seeing her as his Muse. He could even compose and recite poems as he tortures her. A rose-obsessed villain could torture his victims with thorns in all manner of fiendish ways, or choke them on petals, or drown them in rose water. The possibilities are endless.

— Part 2 —
Human Suffering

— Emotions —

Ambition and Greed

He was young and ambitious, with an eye for conquest

Overweening pride and ambition were the ruin of many a man

His ambition would be his downfall

Confidence was one thing, but ego was something else

His ego got in the way of every decision he ever made

There was nothing he would not destroy to feed his ego

Once he knew what we had, he was determined to take it

No cost was too great to achieve his goals, even our lives

Ambition drove his waking moment

Ambition guided him to seek out his dream

He was determined to be the best

Ambition blinded him to the plan's danger

Now was not the time for ego, but cooperation

He was a fool not to question her flattery

She was haughty and prideful

She was far too sure of herself

She aspired to claw her way to the top

Her ambition was to control him utterly

She made men her puppets

She had a ruthless, predatory mind

They underestimated her skills, but not her ambition

She was determined not to let her past hold her back

The man was well-known for greed

His greed had made paupers of us all

His greed devoured all in its path

His greed was a hungry thing

He would not rest until he made his fortune

He regarded our land and its people with greedy eyes

Given half a chance, he would pick us clean

He rubbed his hands together, chortling at his newest acquisition

There was nothing he would not steal

He was a thief and a liar, but somehow charming

Soon, her nimble fingers had pried the object loose from his pocket

Greed had been her undoing

She could not rest until she made the thing hers

Her greed forced her to take more and more risks

Greed was her only lover

The only god she bowed to was greed

Her slim hands caressed the object possessively

Fear and Surprise

His gaze burned with such intensity she felt her soul shiver

The fear was writ large on his unshaven face

His eyes bulged in fright at the thing

Ice shivered down his spine

Cold terror gripped her in its icy embrace

A cold worm of fear gnawed at her spine

Icy tendrils robbed him of action, freezing him in place

He could do nothing but watch, paralyzed with fright

The fear ate away at his sanity, reducing him to a gibbering wreck

It was more than fright, it was a freezing of the soul

Haunted by horror, all she could do was watch helplessly

She dare not do anything for fear of making the wrong decision

He knew one wrong move would cost them their lives

She did not know what to do and so sealed her fate

She felt an agony of despair

Fear knotted inside her

The cold light of fear shone in her eyes

The thought of it tore at her insides

A wave of apprehension washed over her

It gnawed at her like a rat in the guts

The fear beat her down

His heart hammered in his chest

Frightened beyond measure, she ran

Her fear escalated and reason fled

The fear was raw on her face

Her breath caught in her throat

With slowly mounting terror, she realized what he had done

Her relief was short-lived

Soon, the fear returned

She felt impaled by fear, unable to move

The fear choked the scream from her throat

Overcome by fright, she fainted

Nerves rubbed raw, she screamed in terror

His coldness frightened her

Her eyes were frantic headlights of fear

She was torn between anticipation and dread

The fear was eating her alive

Terror shone from her eyes like twin candles of fright

Terror came gasping up her throat in a cold, panting fear

The fear strangled any chance of escape

She fought her fear and lost

Twisted fingers of fear clawed his guts

He was scared, but had to act or all was lost

Fear gave her courage–the courage to see it never happened again

Even faith was no refuge from that awful fear

The raw emotion came spilling out of her in a terrified moan

Eyes wild with fear, her lips desperately called my name

The frantic fear pulsed like a living thing between them

The fear beat in him even louder than his heart

The cold knot of knowing clenched tight

Fear rendered him powerless against the enemy

And in that terrible silence, the fear grew

The fear was a living thing inside her now

Enslaved by fear, all she could was submit

His was a surrender born of fear, not honor

The toxin of terror blazed through his veins

She was trembling, and he had to snap at her to break the trance

Fear stretched like a shadow in the alley of her mind

Startled faces turned, staring at him in fright

Fear flashed through her mind

In a flash of fear, she realized too late

She choked on fear like a fist down her throat

Terror numbed her

Terror slowed her reflexes

The horror was too much for her and she shut her eyes

She recoiled in panic from the grisly scene

A pall of dread hung over her, numbing her to inaction

He instantly became wide awake

The shocking horror slammed into her full force

Her wide eyes looked at him in alarm

His mouth dropped open at the sight of her

She glanced up, startled by the strange noise

His body stiffened in shock

Complete surprise was etched on his face

She stared at him, speechless

Her mouth dropped open in a hushed "O" of surprise

Her voice rose in a shrill of surprise

The shock left him uncertain how to proceed

The shock was too much for her soul to bear

Surprise drained the blood from her face

She jumped at the sound of the sinister voice

A soft gasp of surprise escaped her

Shock and surprise rendered her speechless

She stood there, blank-faced and amazed, as it crept closer

Words failed him

Hate and Revenge

Her eyes grew hot with hate

His eyes bulged with hate

Hate came off him in waves

His voice became ice, cold and sharp as a scalpel

A black curtain of hate fell over his graveyard eyes

He had given into his hate and there was no turning back

The hatred gnawed at him

He lived for nothing more but to kill those he hated

His hatred made him blind

Hate was an ugly thing, and on her, doubly so

The fires of hell stoked the hate in his heart

Only hate lived behind those hell-hot eyes

He let go of his hate only at the moment he died

He carried his hate into death and beyond

Brutal hate and bloody ruin blazed behind those bloodshot eyes

His cruel mouth twisted with hate

His knuckles knotted with hate as he struck the first blow

His blood boiled with the foulness of hate

Every word was contempt, every look hate

The cruelty of his hatred knew no bounds

Day by day, the anger ate at her, nibbling her nerves raw

The fierceness of his hate blazed like a oven

Childhood memories cooked in the juices of his hate

She nursed her hatred like a child

She nursed her hatred like a wound

His hate was an open wound only love could heal

The hatred festered in his thoughts

His hate was a cancer on her life

Those who survived her hate never crossed her again

He released his hatred in a torrent of death

Without his hate, he was nothing

He ate hate the way other men eat breakfast

Her hateful eyes clawed at his heart

She promised through clenched teeth

With mounting rage, he turned on her

His hostile glare was hard as daggers

He choked back anger

The hate was in his voice now, hard and cruel

His voice grew cold, harsh and stony with years of hate

Contempt spilled out of her like an open wound

His contempt shocked her into silence

Spit sprayed and hate flew from his cruel mouth

He raged an endless torrent of abuse at the man

Fists clenched in fury, he stalked forward

The cauldron of her eyes burned with scalding fury

Hate beamed from his eyes like hit-and-run headlights

The old man gloomed and glowered at us from his chair

Hate hardened her heart to his pleas of innocence

Anger burned hell-hot in his gaze

Her heart held grudges her lips dared not speak

Eyes blazing, she slapped his face

His angry voice stabbed the air

His voice cracked hate like a whip

His cruel face twisted in anger

The raw fire of hate blazed in her voice

The wrath was upon him

It was foolish to confront him in this mood

His temper flared and fierce words were spoken

He leveled his icy gaze on her and smiled   but not with his eyes

The smile never touched his eyes

His smile was cold and cruel, just like him

Her chill smile was never touched by the warmth of love

He fed on hate and it festered inside him

The cancer of hate gnawed on his last nerve

Soon, he must explode

And all the while, the hate-bomb ticked inside him, waiting to go off

His fake smile disturbed me because I knew he had always hated me

His hate ignited like arson in his veins

Her hate boiled over in a shrill, punishing tone

Her hands became claws that raked for my face

A storm of sinister emotion rolled across the stranger's face

His anger damned him, yet he could not stop

The cruel flower of hate bloomed in her heart

His hate, the old killing rage, gripped him

A terrible hatred spilled over him and ate at his guts

He hated himself, but projected that hate outward, blaming others

He couldn't stop killing until they were all dead

She hated him and burned for revenge

He would find a way to make them pay—in blood

No prison could cage his hate, nor any asylum sooth his damaged soul

Purple with rage, he vowed revenge

Humiliated and betrayed, her hate turned to poison in her mind

To make them suffer was the sweetest wine

Betrayal was the worst crime of all, and one that must be punished

The fires of revenge kept him warm through the darkness

His vengeance was swift and terrible

The pattern of his vengeance revealed the depths of his hate

His vow was their death

His hate burned on, even after death, so that others took up his cause

She went about her revenge with a singleminded tenacity

The icy road of revenge led her to the slopes of madness

Now, revenge was the only thing left and he reveled in its white-hot fury

Her tortured brain screamed with shrill cries of revenge

Blood demanded blood, and her revenge would be swift

Her heart leapt at the chance to avenge

Vengeance was his lover, hate his only emotion

A wave of hate spilled from the killer—hate and righteous fury

His revenge was her undoing

His vengeance hit home and no one was safe

His eyes bulged with hate and the desire for revenge

Hate guided the avenger's hand

With one last thrust of the blade, his revenge was complete

His heart was black with vengeance

Without the possibility of revenge, her mind sank into despair

Revenge would come, swift and sure

She wanted to hurt him, make him pay

The power of hate drove him like a mighty engine of darkness

The raw wound of her heart demanded revenge

His hatred warred within him

Hatred burnt her bitter soul black

Jealousy and Lust

The jealous green snake of envy hissed in her heart

The cruel worm of jealousy burrowed into her

He wanted all they had and was determined to get it . . .

Jealousy, naked and cruel, gnawed at her thoughts

In a jealous rage, she cursed him and all men

Her jealous nature forbid her from forming close attachments

She had to have everything first or better than her friends

Everything he said or did was misinterpreted by her jealousy

Her jealous heart hungered to possess him, body and soul

If he could not have her, no one could, and the knife would prove it

Her phone blew up with fifty million jealous texts

Jealous and possessive, he was cruel in his affections

He regarded her with insecure, suspicious eyes

The jealousy had driven her mad and there was nothing he could say

She just *knew* he was seeing someone else

Lust burned in his brain and he could think of nothing else

His rage lusted into her with the brute power to possess, to destroy

His fingers yearned to touch her, his mouth to taste her

He had to know what secrets hid inside that soft, yielding flesh

He thought forbidden flesh was the sweetest of all . . .

A lusty feeling of warmth stole over her

Cold eyes caressed her with lusting, invisible fingers

Almost against her will, she began to undress for him

Shame and desire mingled hot in her throat

He had a strange kind of animal magnetism that drew her to him

Bold eyes raked her soft skin, promising pleasure

She was disturbed by the raw power of her attraction to him

She was powerless to resist his foreign charm

She radiated a sinister sensuality that drew men like flies

Blood throbbed in her veins with a scarlet web of desire

He was all she wanted, all she could think about

His pulse quickened with forbidden longing

The glow of desire became a bonfire of lust that consumed them both

A delicious shudder shot through her body

Every inch of her lit up with the burning, urgent need to possess him

His soft words were spoken only in lust, not love

Theirs was a mutual attraction, and a mutual destruction

What they shared was not love, it was madness

Sadness and Despair

Only despair dwelled in the smoking ruins of my soul

Hot tears of shame slid down her rose-colored cheeks

Blinded by tears, the grieving girl ran from him

She gulped back sorrow her eyes could not hide

Sobbing, she begged for forgiveness

Tears fell like rain from her troubled eyes

Tears welled in the bottomless blue pools of her eyes

Her face grew pale and withdrawn at the mention of his name

She bit her lip in dismay at his approach

She bit back tears of grief

No holiday cheer could warm the winter cold from his heart

She wore her sorrow like a shroud

The aching sorrow soured him like an old wound on a rainy day

Overwhelmed by sadness, she collapsed into the chair

The color drained out of her face

The misery finally broke through her fragile control

The sorrow she felt–the guilt–was almost too much to bear

Her throat closed in grief, she could not breathe

Hot tears welled behind her eyes

Desperate tears spilled down her cheeks

With a defeated heart, she put her face in her hands and wept

She was trapped without hope

Anguish stabbed her like a knife

Miserable and alone, she faced the sad truth of her situation

The inner torment was all too visible on her bitter face

He gave a resigned shrug as they led him away

Despair twisted and turned inside her

The torment of his decision kept him up at night

Her heart ached with the loss of her friend

Her dress was somber, her face sunless

Her face was ashen with grief

Her voice was thick with sorrow

The open wound of her soul cried out for relief

The dismal weather did nothing to warm his spirits

A gray light of gloom cast its deathless shadow over her

Sadness weighed heavily on her like a stone she carried on her back

All light and color bleached from her

— Problems —

Alcohol

The wine numbed her and the pills did the rest

Bleary-eyed and boozy, he reached for the bottle like a baby

The captain was well into his cups by then

The liquor smashed all reason from her lips

Though his words were slurred, their meaning was clear

He made to stand, staggered, then sprawled to the piss-stained street

His steps were slow, his speech slurred

The bottle drained, he turned to face me with a look of contempt

His breath reeked of wine and his eyes were unfocused

With a drunken leer, he reached for the front of her dress

He cracked a fresh six-pack, eager to forget

He nursed his brandy and brooded into the night

She cursed and screamed as they tossed her out of the bar

In that lonesome alley, booze-addled brains nursed bottles of death

The drink confused him, made him stumble over his words

Theirs was a night soaked in beer and madness

The beer-soaked night gave way to revulsion in the morning

He drank deep into the night and cursed the dawn

He was dead drunk until he saw the gun, then he was merely dead

Her boozy smile promised more than she could deliver

Fueled by whiskey, the leer on the sailor's face widened

The drink had him in its power and he was useless to her now

The only love his ugly face could get was from a bottle

Greasy lips wrapped tight around the half-empty bottle and sucked

Drunken hands itched to smash her trembling flesh to his

Disease and Disfigurement

Rusty-red blotches marred a once-handsome face

The grim specter of disease haunted his harrowed face

I turned away in disgust at what he'd become

Pus-filled savages, living lepers, they wanted me to eat their disease

The germs ate their flesh, leaving just enough for them to live

The disease spread quickly, reducing the internal organs to mush

A pulpy red paste poured from every orifice

The wound was raw, infected, oozing with putrescent disease

Open sores covered the mewling wretch from head to toe

The disease robbed them of humanity, leaving only monsters behind

The creature drooled disease and its bite was the plague

There were some things that could not be cured

Greasy hands crawling with disease slid over my naked body

Infection shot up her spine and into her brain

The boil burst, splashing blood and pus in a reeking shower

To say she looked ill was an understatement

The fever burned into his brain

Hands covered in festering scabs reached out of the darkness

The hollows of her cheeks were purple with spider-veins

His brain bubbled with disease, dancing with microscopic madness

It was a plague of pus, a storm of sores for which there was no cure

The creep's shuffling feet and reedy cough made me sick

The swelling grew until I could barely move

His red-rimmed eyes burned with the madness of the plague

The mad scientist's needle filled her with every horror known to man

A disgusting yellow fluid leaked from his eyes and nose

The whip welts were angry pink lines against her otherwise perfect skin

Dozens of skin grafts left him looking like a human jigsaw puzzle

His acne scars ran so deep, they were like moon craters

His spit sprayed, germs squirting into my mouth with every shout

A million microbes lurked in every inch of that dripping orifice

The twisted beggar pawed at me with dirty hands and roving eyes

He picked at his scabs and reached for my sandwich

He scratched at the open sore on his neck, drawing blood

Burst blisters crawled across his lips like ants to a picnic

Putrid hearts propelled crooked limbs in a mad rush to infect me

The freak crept closer, dragging his heavy clubfoot behind him

He shook the scarred stump of his wrist at me in warning

His body was a crusted ruin of picked scabs and yellow pus

Bloodshot eyes peered dully from his ravaged face

Withered and bruised by burst veins, her skin was patchwork horror

He longed to put his disease into her and watch her die

The disease had run its course, leaving him a twisted wreck

Drugs

Not even the ghostly rattling of chains could wake me from my drug-induced slumber

The needle's pinch gave sweet relief from the pain of life

The drug robbed her of all reason

Under its chemical spell, she felt she could do anything

The room spun and the floor rose up to meet him

Senses swimming, she knew she'd been drugged

The junkie shivered and shook, feeble for his next fix

Her limbs were unclean, a network of scabs and collapsed veins

His arms were scarred by his addiction

One dose and he could forget, if only for a few hours

Escape was only a needle away . . .

The oblivion he sought was found at the end of a needle

The drug had made a living skeleton of her once-great beauty

I recoiled from the monster the drug had made her

There was no salvation in his addiction, only death

One more "fix" fixed nothing

The drug had him now—and with it, mastery of his soul

Shifty-eyed, the junkie licked her lips and reached for his wallet

The drug danced in her veins, singing songs no sober mind could hear

The peace of the needle gave way to the peace of the grave

The tourniquet was a comforting presence around his arm

The need for her next fix wasn't far behind

Nausea, Fainting, and Vomiting

Reason fled, along with the contents of his stomach

Barf-coated lips begged for mercy

The vomit steamed out of him like gasoline on a bonfire

Slime-soaked in his own vomit, he prayed for death

The barf boiled out of him in a waterfall of revulsion

He spat hot vomit in a sea of horror

The contents of his stomach upended on the floor

Hot vomit showered her senseless

Barf-blasted and beaten, he lay down to die

Her hair was slimed to the toilet, trapped by her own vomit

Barf bubbled out of him like hot stink on tap

The vomit formed a chunky brown pool at his feet

She closed her eyes and retched

There was blood in his barf, a sticky red oatmeal

He blew barf-covered kisses at her as they hauled him away

Through bitter tears and barf-breath, he confessed his crime

She looked away, sick at the sight of him

A gruesome feeling of regret washed over him

The horror was too much and she turned away

Pale and feverish, she turned away in disgust

She covered her mouth so only a little vomit leaked through

He averted his eyes and leaned against the wall

Through the blood and stench, he felt himself sicken

A burning wave of nausea poured over her

She clutched at her belly and doubled over

She cursed me through barf-crusted lips

The barf was slick on her tongue as she drunkenly kissed me

He drank until the vomit splashed out of him

Through vomit-flecked lips, the man muttered a furtive prayer

One look at that ghastly scene and she swooned to the ground

She felt faint, feverish

She collapsed in a dead faint

The shock of it sent her swooning

Utterly repulsed, she let the faint sweep her away from that awful scene

The musk of life, the stink of death, all became one in her

There was a smell of rot that pierced the senses

He smelled like an armpit dipped in earwax

The bum smelled of the sewer and forgotten dreams

There was at once a smell of sickness and despair

The very air itself recoiled from that noisome stench

A hazy, reeking fog hung over the place and I was eager to dispel it

The hideous smell assailed my nostrils

The reeking pit was piled high with bodies left to rot in the noonday sun

His breath smelled like an open sewer and his words were no better

A rich, woolen haze blanketed me, its scent my first taste of death

No city dump could compare to the smell of that godless crypt

The unwashed stench of the blubbery freak was like an armpit from hell

The city stank of bodies shimmering in the soup of their own sweat

— Part 3 —
Man Against Nature

— ELEMENTAL FURY —

Cold and Ice

A numbness crept over him, not just from the cold, but the memory

The frost had taken his fingers, but not his pride

The frostbitten hands were black and mottled from exposure

An icy chill swept down and with it, with the first dusting of snow

The blizzard howled, but not so fiercely as the beast he fought

The avalanche threatened to bury them in an icy tomb

There was snow in the air and terror on her mind

The snow crunched underfoot as they led me to the gallows

His foot crashed through the ice to the freezing pond below

The glare of sun on snow had made him blind

Snow-blind, he staggered across the frozen waste

The once-pure snow had turned to sickly brown slush

He cursed the cold outside and the message that drew him from his bed

Cursing, he stamped his feet and blew on his hands to warm them

The icy road gave him fits as he drove to work

A frost had fallen across the land, bringing with it the chill of the grave

She sniffled and tried to smile, crossing her arms for warmth

He stamped snow from his boots, glad to be coming in from the cold

The cold was in him, freezing him beyond all worldly cares

Icy fingers seduced him to lie down, to give in to the storm

The snow sealed us in

Earth and Stone

The ground soon turned to mud

Mud sucked at his heels as he slogged across the swampy ground

Mud-spattered and sodden, she barricaded herself in the tiny cabin

Wet earth clung to him

There was mud on his boots, but he said he hadn't left the house all day

The ground was hard, frozen, and impossible to dig a grave in

He shoveled dirt and hoped no one would find the body

He was covered in grave-grime and walked on unsteady legs

The open grave gaped wide, ready to receive him

With each passing shovelful of earth, the grave widened

The weathered stone was old, crumbling

The pioneer's tombstone was pitted and worn, barely readable

A broken-winged angel judged me with unseeing stone eyes

The strange statue greeted me with welcoming arms and sinister smile

The mountain's terrible stone face glared down at him

Climbing the mountain had kept us safe from what waited below

One misstep and the mountain's judgment would be swift and brutal

A thousand feet of unyielding stone towered over him

The high stone wall's top had razors of broken glass cemented into it

The quarry was a vast, rocky wasteland

The quarry was a wound in the earth that bled stone

The dusty ground was cracked and broken, parched of all life

Dust puffed up with each step

Heat and Flame

A fluttering, flickering flame was Death's only light

The match flared, and in that moment, she saw her death

The flame flickered, dimmed low as if hushed by a ghostly whisper

Hell-hot, the forest fire raged

It was an arsonist's dream, an image of hell

The city burned, a sea of black and orange against the night sky

Dying, the fireplace hissed and sputtered

Orange embers were the room's only light

When the fire died, all hope would die with it

The candles dimmed and bowed to the wind

A sudden breeze snuffed the candle out, plunging her into darkness

The warm fire comforted them against the night's horrors

He threw another log on the fire with a grunt of satisfaction

He prodded the logs with a long iron poker

The fireplace was the only defense from the freezing horror outside

The black candles were lit at each point of the pentagram

The red wax melted like blood

The candle burned low

She fumbled with the candle and wax splashed her hand

The church walls glittered with the tiny flames of a hundred candles

The flames guttered and died in that awful wind

She placed scented candles around the bathtub and relaxed

The fire lit, he stepped back in relief

Her pale face glowed orange-yellow in the firelight

The wet wood smoked but would not catch fire

He thumbed his lighter and prayed

She flicked the lighter wheel and orange flame sprang up

He struck a match and the tiny flame revealed the truth

The summer heat cooked him in his business suit

The blazing sun bore down on him relentlessly

The sun's warmth stood out in stark contrast to the chill horror

Hot sand burning bare feet, she ran for the cool ocean water

The beach swam in a sultry haze of shimmering yellow heat

The brutal desert sun baked down

The sky was an oven

The desert was a ghastly furnace that burned my dying soul

The sun glared like an open wound in the sky

The desert sands were a vast dune sea

The shifting sands swallowed any hope of survival

The sun was sinking, taking all hope and warmth with it

A vast ball of yellow fire hung in the pure blue sky

The dawn sky revealed the night's horrors

The dim, gray light of dawn filtered through the warm darkness

The sun climbed the sky like a king with a fiery crown

The air was humid, the temperature soaring

The air was thick, muggy, and I began to sweat

The volcano erupted, sending boiling lava toward the village

The volcanic crater smoked and steamed in the dying light

Jackson Dean Chase

Night and Shadow

There was a furtive movement of black on black

He moved like one of night's many shadows

Darkness clung to him like a shroud

The night was alive with the sounds of death

Clinging to the darkness, he was careful not to be seen

From the shadows, the night whispered secret terrors

A sinister shadow detached itself from the darkness

A living shadow stepped into my path

He moved swiftly through the fog

He melted into darkness

He melded with the shadows

He became one with the darkness

The darkness was a living thing

The night held terror

Despite the darkness, he saw just enough to know he was in trouble

From the darkness, they fell upon them, sweeping down like wolves

A gash of crimson-purple twilight smashed the sun from the sky

Purple-black twilight crushed the sun from the sky

Darkness lay over the land

The sun fell and shadows were born

Night fell, and with it came terror

She called for help, and the darkness answered back

The silver moon shone down on a scene of horror

The moon's uncaring eye watched the horror unfold

The crescent moon clawed the night sky

Black clouds hid the moon in a sea of night

One by one, the stars winked out and the horror began

The moon-drenched sky gave everything an eerie glow

They were barricaded by bonds of night

The air was thick with the glooming of night

Inky shadows moved through the forest's gloom

There was nothing for it now but to wait the break of day

We huddled near the fire and cursed the dark

I vowed this night would end in my death—or theirs

Water and Wind

Lightning struck and in that terrible flash, the truth was revealed

Thunder boomed and the sky grew dark

Thunder rolled across the land like the haunted images in her mind

The storm raged and lightning struck nearer each time

The storm was one step ahead of us

It was hopeless to evade the gathering storm

Storm clouds gathered overhead, black and terrible

There was no end to the storm that raged outside

The storm's power passed and little by little, the sun came out

The storm lashed out at us with all its fury

The tornado was a tunnel of death from which none survived

The tornado picked up houses and cars like child's toys

Waves crashed against the shore, swelling dark and deadly

The ocean drank the sky, feeding from its fury

The storm passed, but not without cost

Waves lashed the ship's deck, threatening to throw me overboard

Roaring waves crashed over the deck

The storm guided our ship toward the reef and into hell

A watery grave awaited all who sailed this night

The sky was grim, gray with the first drops of rain

Overhead, the sky was gloom-gray, threatening rain

The black clouds clashed with the slate of the sky

The colorless sky promised rain

The wet sky was gray and friendless, like me

Puddles of icy water led from the porch into the house

The rains came and washed clean the horror

Rain poured down in sheets, soaking me to the bone

I felt the chill before the first drops fell

Rain fell from an angry sky

— DON'T START WITH WEATHER OR SETTING —

Old stories often begin with lengthy descriptions of setting and weather (e.g., *"It was a dark and stormy night in the quiet town of Haddonfield, Illinois."*). This no longer works. Today's readers, agents, and editors will throw your book away if they see that.

So what's the best way to open a story? Hook your reader with the main character saying or doing something intriguing (e.g., *"Snake Samson drove his fist into the madman's face."* Build on that, then you can (briefly) work in the setting and weather.

Rain swept the people from the streets like a liquid broom

The sky wept at my folly

Drenched and alone, I wandered the wet gray wilderness

The sky was gloom-gray, wet with bitter rain

The sky's belly slit open and rained her children upon them

The wind whipped, plucking at her robe with icy fingers

The wind howled at her loss

There was fear in that breeze, the first whiff of death

The wind moaned in misery

The dismal wind sent a chill up my spine

The wind blew through that barren place like a lost child

The breeze brought death

The cold wind of death sang through that awful place

A wind like a funeral dirge carried her name upon its wings

Invisible wings beat about our heads

Cold wind, gray sky, and work to be done

A chill wind of longing swept over her

The gray wind chilled me

The gathering clouds angry grew against the light

A savage wind tore the umbrella from my hand

My soul was sick at the thought of another gray day filled with rain

The ashen sky opened up

The first gray drops of rain fell on my cheek

The wind moaned like a lost child

A bitter wind howled from the ghoul-gray sky

— WILDLIFE —

Animals

Bear claws made a dripping ruin of his face

The grizzly bear's slavering jaws slammed down

The brown bear reared up, bellowing rage

The polar bear charged, black eyes promising death

The tiger's teeth clamped down and would not let go

Black lips pulled back from ivory fangs in the tiger's mouth

The tiger was a flashing nightmare of black and orange

The lion's jaws salivated at the thought of its feast

The lion unsheathed its killing claws

The lion roared its rage

The panther glided forward on paws of night

The big cat prowled silently

Hungry green eyes peered from the panther's skull

Silent and relentless, the big cat stalked her

The wolf gave a mournful howl and the moon answered back

Hot on his heels, the pack bayed for his blood

The wolf loped forward, hungry for the kill

Hair raised and ears back, the house cat hissed

The cat was wild, feral, and regarded me with hateful gold eyes

The cat's claws dug bloody furrows in my arm

The tomcat yowled and screeched

The cat watched me with knowing eyes

Whatever secrets the cat knew, she kept to herself

The Doberman growled and padded forward, teeth bared

The pit bull's teeth were like a vise on my ankle

The hounds snarled and snapped at his heels

The little dog whimpered and whined for its dead master

The shaggy dog's fur was matted with blood

The poor dog was skittish, like it had been kicked one too many times

The pup licked my hand, then quickly looked over its shoulder in alarm

Bats and Birds

Raven wings beat the sky black

In a furious flapping of wings, the eagle descended

The eagle screamed, a deadly diving mass of claws and feathers

The falcon took aim at her eyes, plucking the dusky jewels from her skull's grasp

With a vicious nod, the bird's dripping beak pecked out her eye

The evil bird blinked at me, then bit down on my thumb

Vultures circled overhead, flying tombstones that marked my death

The vulture's beak stripped the flesh from the dead man's bones

The parrot spoke better English than its master

The parrot croaked the killer's name

The parrot croaked the last words of its master

The seagulls picked at the ghastly remains in that watery hell

In a beating of leathery wings, the bats were upon us

Overhead, the bats formed a ceiling of fur and leather

The bloodsucking bats chittered and flapped over the horse carcass

The vampire bat lapped the nectar of life from his neck

Guano dropped from the cave ceiling, and I swear, the bat laughed

Reptiles

The snake struck, twin fangs flashing like knives

The serpent slithered, its forked tongue seeking the scent

The cobra swayed up from the temple floor

The cobra's hood unfurled

Deadly tight, the python's coils squeezed

Sunlight glistened black and gold off the anaconda's scaly skin

A serpentine rattling alerted me to the snake's presence

The angry rattler sank its fangs into the girl's ankle

The crocodile's jaws snapped shut

The crocodiles' mouths were like twin beds of nails

The crocodile knifed through the water, silent and deadly

The alligator's jaws crunched down, its body thrashed, and the child disappeared beneath the churning red waters

The alligator's scaly tail slapped me back in a crushing blow

The big lizard looked like it would eat anything

Its tiny dinosaur brain regarded me as nothing more than its next meal

The curious lizard watched me with rotating eyes

Vermin

Spider webs clung to my hair as I pushed my way forward

The hairy spiders crawled over her naked body

One bite from those tiny jaws meant agony

It grabbed my skin between black mandibles and chewed

Gnashing, gnawing mandibles knifed into his skin

The bug bites itched and burned like mad

The crawling carpet of army ants marched relentlessly toward us

Poison dripped from the spider's clacking fangs

In a panic, she brushed at the bloodsucking leeches covering her legs

The insect laid its eggs in his brain while he slept

The worms oozed out of him like spaghetti from hell

Centipedes—as fat as my fist and long as my arm—carpeted the jungle

Lice crawled over her scalp like dandruff from hell

Maggots had made short work of the corpse

The air was black with the buzzing of flies

The fly buzzed, regarding me with dull red eyes

The defiant rat regarded me with beady red eyes

The hungry rats swarmed over the body

Rats gnawed his mangled limbs

With a terrified squeak, the rat fled

The rat's fur was filthy, crawling with disease

The sewer tunnel was choked by a horde of ravenous rats

Rats poured from the tunnel, desperate to escape

Water Predators (Non-Reptilian)

The shark's black eyes knew only hunger

Rows of deadly teeth sliced and snacked on the unfortunate diver

A bullet-faced killer knifed through the crimson water

The sharks swarmed, feasting in their frenzy

The shark-infested waters ran red with meat and gore

A shark's fin broke the surface

Shark fins circled the survivors

The sharks swarmed forward, hungry for the kill

Beneath me, I saw the sliding black shadow and knew I was not alone

The hammerhead circled, hoping for an easy meal

The great white was just as big and ugly as my ex-wife—and twice as dangerous

The squid's tentacles dragged me closer to its snapping beak

The rubbery tentacles gripped me as no sermon could

Jetting ink, the octopus spun away in a web of night

The eel's needle-like teeth were a junkie's paradise

The crab's claws dug the meat from his eyes

The crab scuttled forward, claws clacking

The fish nibbled him until nothing was left

The piranha made short work of the body

The piranha darted forward, teeth snapping

The river was packed with piranha, each mouth a tiny engine of death

The piranha gathered and gorged on the blood-red feast

— PART 4 —
Words of Power

— Hell's Coloring Book —

By mixing colors with other words and/or doubling-up similar shades, you can quickly come up with powerful descriptions, such as "the October sky was ghoul-gray" or "the starless night was steeped in shadow."

Black

Anthracite, black pearl, blue-black, coal, crow, dark, dead, ebony, ink, jet, midnight, moonless, night, obsidian, onyx, pitch, raven, sable, shadow, starless, Stygian, subterranean, tenebrous, void, unlit

Blue

Air Force, azure, baby, cerulean, cobalt, cornflower, electric blue, delft, federal, ice, indigo, lapis lazuli, marine, midnight blue, navy, neon, ocean, peacock, periwinkle, powder, Prussian, robin's egg, royal, sapphire, sea-blue, sky, slate blue, sorrowful, steel, teal, turquoise, ultramarine, wedgewood

Brown/Beige

Bay, brick, bronze, brunette, buckskin, café au lait, caramel, chestnut, chocolate, cinnamon, cocoa, coffee, copper, drab, dun, earth, ecru, fawn, foxy, ginger, hazel, henna, khaki, mahogany, maple, mocha, mud, mushroom, nut brown, nutmeg, pecan, raisin, roan, rosewood, saddle, sepia, tan, tanned, taupe, tawny, toffee, tortoise shell, umber, walnut

Gray

Ashen, bleak, charcoal, cloudy, dismal, dove, drab, dreary, dull, gloomy, grizzled, gunmetal, hoary, iron, murky, overcast, pearl, sickly, silver, slate gray, smoky, sooty, somber, stone, sunless, tattletale, tombstone

Green

Aqua, aquamarine, bluish-green, celadon, chartreuse, emerald, envy, forest, grassy, hunter, jade, jealous, kelly, leaf, lime, malachite, mist, mold, moss, olive, pea, pine, sea-green, verdant

Orange

Amber-orange, apricot, atomic tangerine, bittersweet, burnt orange, carrot, champagne, coral, deep carrot, flame, lion, orange peel, orange-red, peach, pumpkin, safety orange, sunset, tangelo, tangerine

Purple

Açai, amaranth, amethyst, aubergine, azurite, blackberry, bluebell, crocus, eggplant, electric purple, frostbite, fuchsia, heliotrope, hibiscus, imperial, indigo, lavender, lilac, lotus, magenta, mauve, orchid, pinot noir, plum, psychedelic, royal, thistle, Tyrian, violet, wisteria

Red/Pink

Apple, auburn, beet, blood, brass, brick, burgundy, candy apple, cardinal, carmine, cerise, cherry, cinnamon, cinnabar, claret, cochineal, crimson, currant, dusky rose, fire, fire engine, fulvous, garnet, hellish, lobster, maroon, ox-blood, raspberry, red amber, rose, rosy, rubescent, rubicund, ruddy, ruby, russet, rust, salmon, sanguine, scarlet, shrimp, strawberry, terra cotta, Titian, Tyrian, tomato, vermeil, vermilion, wine

White/Off-White

Alabaster, anemic, bleached, bloodless, chalk, colorless, cream, deathly, drained, drawn, ecru, eggshell, ghostly, ivory, lily, magnolia, milky, milky quartz, moon, moonstone, oatmeal, opal, oyster, pale, pallid, parchment, pasty, peaked, pinched, salt-and-pepper, snow, vanilla, virgin, wan, washed out, waxen, white jade

Yellow/Gold

Amber, ash blonde, blonde, brass, burnished, buff, cadmium, daffodil, flaxen, fool's gold, fulvous, golden, honey, lemon, jaundiced, jonquil, mustard, palomino, platinum, primrose, sallow, sandy, silver-blonde, straw, tawny, wheat, white-gold

— COLORS WRITING EXERCISE —

Experiment with your own word/color combinations and use them in a descriptive tag. Come up with at least five for each color and feel free to mix-and-match colors (e.g., yellow and brown could be combined as "Her *wheat*-colored hair fell in waves over slim, *tanned* shoulders").

— Vocabulary of Death —

How many times have you been stumped trying to come up with clever ways to say how a character was injured, knocked out or killed? That's why I came up with my "Vocabulary of Death." Use it for inspiration the next time writer's block wraps its fearsome fingers around your brain!

Acid and Drowning

Bubble, blister, boil, burn, consume, corrode, crumble, damage, destroy, dissolve, disintegrate, decay, eat away/into/through, erode, immerse, inhale, liquify, scald, sear, sizzle, soak, submerge, wear away

Biting and Blood-Drinking

Ate, bit, bite, bolt down, breakfast, chew, chomp, chow down, chug, consume, crunch, demolish, devour, dine, dispose of, drink, eat, fang, feast, feed, gnaw, gobble, gorge, graze, gulp, guzzle, ingest, lunch, munch, nibble, nip, nosh, partake of, pig out on, polish off, put away, quaff, scarf, sip, snack, snap, swallow, swill, swig, sup, tear, tuck into

Crushing

Bang, bash, batter, beat, belt, bludgeon, bop, brain, break, bounce, bump, burst, bust, butt, clout, clobber, collide, crack, crease, crumple, crunch, crush, dent, flatten, force, fracture, fragment, grate, grind, hammer, hit, impact, kick, knock, mangle, mash, paste, pound, press, pry, pulp, pulverize, pummel, punch, ram, sap, slam, slap, smash, smack, smite, smoosh, smush, snap, sock, splinter, squash, squeeze, strike, thump, trample, thwack, wallop, whack, wham

Cutting and Clawing

Bleed, carve, chop, claw, clip, crop, cube, cut, cut to pieces/to ribbons, dice, engrave, etch, fell, gash, graze, incise, knife, lacerate, mince, mow, nick, pincer, rake, rend, rip, saw, scratch, score, shred, slash, slice, slit, sliver, snip, split, strip, talon, tatter, tear, trim, whittle

Fire, Electrocution, Explosions, and Guns

Ablaze, aflame, alight, bag, bake, blacken, blast, blaze, blister, blow up, bomb, bombard, bonfire, brand, broil, burn, burst, candle, careen, char, charge, detonate, discharge, emit, fire, flame, flare, electrify, electrocute, erupt, explode, fly, fly apart, glow, go up in flames, gun down, ignite, incinerate, jolt, juice, launch, let fly, let loose, let off, light, lit, mow down, open fire, pick off, ping, plug, pot shot, pump full of lead, ricochet, roar, roast, rocket, sear, scald, scorch, set off, shock, shoot, shoot down, shrapnel, singe, sizzle, smoke, smolder, snipe, streak, vaporize, went up in flames, whistle, whiz, whoosh, wing, zap, zip

Killer and Victim Vocalizations

Babble, bark, bawl, bay, bellow, blubber, blurt out, breathe, burble, cackle, call for help, call out, caterwaul, chant, cheer, choke, chortle, chuckle, cough, cry, cry out, curse, exclaim, exhale, gabble, gag, gargle, gasp, gibber, giggle, grate, groan, growl, grumble, grunt, guffaw, gulp, gurgle, holler, hoot, howl, inhale, intone, invoke, jabber, keen, lament, laugh, mewl, moan, mumble, murmur, mutter, purr, rasp, roar, sing, scream, screech, shout, shriek, shrill, sigh, snap, snarl, snicker, snigger, snivel, sob, squeak, strangle, tee-hee, titter, twitter, wail, weep, wheeze, whimper, whine, whisper, whistle, yell, yelp, yowl

Murder and Execution

Annihilate, assassinate, bump off, butcher, croak, cut down, destroy, dispatch, dispose of, do away with, do in, eliminate, end, execute, exterminate, extinguish, finish, finish off, ice, kill, knock off, liquidate, massacre, murder, neutralize, polish off, put to death, rub out, slaughter, slay, snuff, take/end life, take out, terminate, waste, whack

Piercing

Bayonet, bore through, chisel, drill through, feed, finger, force, fork, gouge, gore, harpoon, hole, horn, impale, inject, insert, jab, knife, lance, needle, penetrate, perforate, pierce, pin, pincushion, point, poke, plug, punch, prick, puncture, push, run through, skewer, spear, spike, stab, stick, sting, transfix

Strangling and Fainting

Asphyxiate, black out, choke, choke out, collapse, conk out, cut off air, cut off breath, dizzy, fall unconscious, gag, gasp, go out like a light, gurgle, faint, fight for air, fight for breath, hang, keel over, knock out, light-headed, loss of consciousness, pass out, smother, stifle, strangle, suffocate, swoon, throttle, unsteady, woozy

Violent Release of Bodily Fluids, Guts, and Organs

Barf, bleed, blob, bloom, blossom, boil, bubble, burst, cascade, deluge, discharge, downpour, drain, dribble, drip, drizzle, drool, drop, dump, eject, emanate, empty, escape, evacuate, excrete, explode, extract, exude, filter, flood, flow, flower, fountain, gag, gargle, geyser, glob, glop, gloop, gob, goop, gurgle, gush, heave, issue, jet, leak, ooze, outflow, outpour, plop, pool, pour, puddle, puke, radiate, rain, ralph, ran, release, remove, retch, river, rush, secrete, seep, shot, slime, sluice, slurp, spill, splash, spat, spatter, spew, splatter, spot, spout, spurt, storm, stream, surge, swam, sweat, tear, torrent, trickle, unleash, unload, upchuck, well out/well up from, void, vomit

Violent Removal of Body Parts and Skin

Amputate, behead, came away/off, carve, chop, cut away/off, decapitate, disembowel, dismember, eviscerate, flay, flew away/off, flog, grab, gut, hack, harvest, hew, lash, lop off, pare, part, peel, pluck, pull, prune, pry, remove, rip, scourge, seize, sever, shave, shear, skin, slice, snatch, snip off, strip away, tear away/off, tug, whip, wrench, yank

— Vocabulary Writing Exercise —

Create at least five exciting tags for each category using the vocabulary words (in any tense). Feel free to use multiple words and/or mix-n-match from different categories (e.g., for piercing: "He *groaned* as the spear *punched* past his ribs and *pricked* a lung").

ABOUT THE AUTHOR

Jackson Dean Chase brings you Bold Visions of Dark Places. He lives in Seattle and is the author of thirteen books, including six #1 bestsellers and the action-packed dystopian thriller, *Drone*.

Did you enjoy this book?

If you did, please leave an online review. Even if it's just a few lines, your words will help this book reach new readers.

Have a question or suggestion? Or just want to say hi?

Friend or follow him—Jackson loves to connect with his fans!

Website: JacksonDeanChase.com

Facebook: facebook.com/jacksondeanchase

Tumblr: jacksondeanchase.tumblr.com

Twitter: @Jackson_D_Chase

Email: jackson@jacksondeanchase.com

Want to know when Jackson's next book is coming out?

Sign up at **www.JacksonDeanChase.com** to get **FREE** books and the latest news. There's NO SPAM, and your email address will never be sold or shared.

Thank you for buying the ACTION WRITERS' PHRASE BOOK!

READY TO WRITE LIKE THE PROS?

ESSENTIAL REFERENCE for All Authors of Horror, Dark Fantasy, Paranormal, Thrillers & Urban Fantasy.

OVER 3,000 EVIL WAYS to Describe Death, Gore, Maniacs, Monsters & More!

STOP WRITER'S BLOCK and Be More Creative Now.

HORROR WRITERS' PHRASE BOOK
JACKSON DEAN CHASE

Prepare to be scared! Horror expert Jackson Dean Chase serves up a bone-chilling feast of ghosts, ghouls, and gore in the *Writers' Phrase Book* that started it all. Great for novels, short stories, and fan fiction!

eBook and Trade Paperback available now

NUKE WRITERS' BLOCK FOREVER!

STOP WRITERS' BLOCK and Be More Creative Now!

ESSENTIAL REFERENCE for All Authors of Apocalyptic, Post-Apocalyptic, Dystopian, Prepper and Zombie Fiction

4,000+ RADIOACTIVE WAYS to describe the End of the World with Aliens, Mutants, Plague, Robots, Weapons and More!

POST-APOCALYPSE WRITERS' PHRASE BOOK

JACKSON DEAN CHASE

Author of the HORROR WRITERS' PHRASE BOOK

Writing so hot, it's radioactive! Don't be caught dead without this book if you're an author of apocalyptic, post-apocalyptic, dystopian, prepper, or zombie fiction!

eBook and Trade Paperback available now

Special Thanks

Authors are nowhere without their fans, and I'd like to extend my special thanks to some of the best on the planet:

    Tiffany Archer   Dianne Bylo
    Crystal Carter   Jen Crews
    David Karner   Melanie Marsh
    Sherry Rentschler Tina Simon
    Julie Stafford

Would you like your name thanked in a future book and other cool perks? Go to **www.JacksonDeanChase.com**, sign up for your **FREE** books, then join my Facebook Group, to learn how to become part of my **Launch Team**!

As a **Launch Team** member, you'll be eligible to read my new books before anyone else, plus you'll receive even more **FREE** books as a special bonus. *(Offer subject to change without notice.)*

www.JacksonDeanChase.com

Printed in Great Britain
by Amazon